THE
F.O.R.C.E.

POWERFUL STRATEGIES FOR TEENS AND YOUNG PEOPLE TO REACH THE AMERICAN DREAM

SHAWN NOROUZIAN

The F.O.R.C.E.: Powerful Strategies for Teens and Young People to Reach the American Dream, Published October, 2016

Editorial and Proofreading Services: Jenna Lloyd, Kathy Bruins, Karen Grennan
Interior Layout and Cover Design: Howard Johnson
Photo Credits: Part opener flag: United States waving flag, designed by Freepik.com
Chapter opener flag: Happy labor day card, designed by Freepik.com
Front Cover: Abstract Illustration of American Flag, Image ID: 231205804, Shutterstock
Author photo: © Shawn Norouzian

SDP Publishing

Published by SDP Publishing, an imprint of SDP Publishing Solutions, LLC.

For more information about this book contact Lisa Akoury-Ross by email at lross@SDPPublishing.com.

To obtain permission(s) to use material from this work, please submit a written request to:

SDP Publishing
Permissions Department
36 Captain's Way, East Bridgewater, MA 02333
or email your request to info@SDPPublishing.com.

ISBN-13 (print): 978-0-9981277-1-2
e-ISBN-13 (ebook): 978-0-9981277-2-9
Library of Congress Control Number: 2016954446

Printed in the United States of America

This book is dedicated to America's younger generation who are willing to work hard and help one another to reach the American Dream. Opportunities exist of which you may or may not be aware. This book's goal is to bring you awareness and encourage you not to take these opportunities for granted. I strongly believe in you! Use the F.O.R.C.E. inside you to be more dedicated and motivated seeing that all dreams are possible.

ACKNOWLEDGMENTS

First and foremost, I want to thank my parents in heaven who made extreme sacrifices by letting their young teenage son go to follow his dreams without knowing if they would ever see him again. Your model of courage will live on through me.

My brother Reza deserves many thanks for being there through thick and thin as well as my valuable friends, my wife, and children.

I also must thank Dr. Deleon who inspired me to start writing this book, and believed in my philosophy to help the society on a grand scale.

Last but not least, I want to thank my publisher, Lisa Akoury-Ross of SDP Publishing; and editors Jenna Lloyd and Kathy Bruins for bringing my story and philosophy to life; and Howard Johnson for his creative cover and interior layout designs. Thank you all for helping me reach the finish line in a meaningful way.

TABLE OF CONTENTS

PART 1

MY JOURNEY

INTRODUCTION

The main objective for every human being is to be successful and enjoy true freedom. I am here as a living example to say that in America, this goal is attainable. My story will inspire you to remember there are countless opportunities for those who seek and work for them.

The life lessons I have learned during the thirty-eight years since my arrival to the U.S.A., I have decided to share for I believe it will encourage you to not settle for mediocre living. My story along with a unique philosophy called F.O.R.C.E. that I have developed throughout the years is meant to help the younger generation of this great nation. Any pre-teens, teens, and young adults reading this book will become more aware and APPRECIATE ALL OPPORTUNITIES you have living in America. You have the power to provide positive influence as you go through these critical developmental years and beyond! Every one of us has a force within that drives us on a daily basis. You can use your inner force to get you anywhere in life you desire. If the negative force is used, we all know where that leads; however, if my simple, positive force is used, you will reach the American Dream.

Young people, do you know that your loved ones and those that truly care for you are a great resource when you are looking for answers and solutions in life? No one cares for you as much as trustworthy people you know; they will prevent you from wandering off toward wrong paths. Remembering my teenage years, I realize more than ever the importance of keeping positive connections with those who have your best interests in mind.

I also intend to set up a foundation in order to contribute a portion of the proceeds from this book to different causes that would help the quality of life for hungry children and teens who need help to survive and gain higher education. I was given much and now it's my turn to give. As you grow, may you also be given the rich opportunity of giving back.

Remember where you come from as you walk forward to a life full of the American Dream.

1
THE JOURNEY TO USA

The moment I stepped into that massive 747 bound for America, I felt a sense of anxiousness wash over me. My face felt warm, my chest heavy, and the air thick. The closer I moved toward my seat, the more I fought the urge to turn and push my way out the door. I looked back at my brother, Abe, for guidance and he motioned for me to move forward. Even though every muscle in my fourteen-year-old body wanted to run back to the safety of my parents, I knew I had to keep going. Once I found our row, I slid into my seat and struggled to put on the seatbelt. The beads of sweat running down my face, and my heart trying to burst out of my chest, made me realize how afraid I was to fly.

The look on Abe's face showed he was just as nervous as

me. Other than what our parents and a few family members had shared with us, neither of us truly understood what moving to America really meant or what our new lives would hold.

I began to shake as I felt the jet engines rumble. Abe kept telling me that it would be alright, but seeing his eyes well up, I understood that he was repeating it as much for himself as for me. At twenty-two, he was not only leaving behind our parents, but his new wife too, at least temporarily. Our tears streamed as the plane gathered speed down the runway. As afraid as I was to fly that first time, I worried more about what we faced moving to a country where we did not even speak the language.

I knew my parents struggled with the choice to send me to live in a faraway land without them for they were obviously upset. In the weeks before we left, my mother told us how they believed sending us to America was the only way to give us greater opportunities in life.

Our brother, Reza, was sent to the U.S. a year earlier. He lived with friends who invited him there in Indiana. Since Reza was eighteen, he could be my legal guardian. Once we arrived in America, Reza would play the role of mother, father, uncle, and other members of our close-knit family.

Having survived takeoff, Abe and I relaxed a bit and found ourselves distracted by the incredible views from the plane. In 1978, flying was much different than it is now. The flight attendants offered a selection of food and beverages and cheerfully accommodated every request. Even though I was scared, the experience was memorable.

While Abe seemed to have forgotten his initial fear, I wondered when I would see my family again. I also worried about what my life would be like. I really had no idea what to expect. The only thing certain was that I had to continue my education. The longer we were on the plane, the more I fell into a state of shock. Barely a teenager, all I wanted was to have fun with my friends and live a carefree life. Instead, I was traveling to a foreign land to build a new life. My parents had told me that America was the best country in the world to continue my education, but I had no clue what that really meant.

Our flight seemed to go on forever. Fortunately, the flight attendants on our way to New York did speak Farsi. After noticing how upset we were initially, they checked on us often, which made me feel better. Although I wondered what would become of us once we arrived in America, Abe and I still made the best of our time in the air.

We landed at New York's JFK Airport late in the afternoon, exhausted from the 18-hour flight. Abe and I were in this enormous airport in one of the largest cities in the world. We had no idea where to go and couldn't read a single sign. Plus, we needed to find a restroom. Abe had to go very bad. By the figures on the signs and people walking in and out, we were able to find the restrooms. To our surprise, each stall required a dime to pay to use the toilet. We didn't have any dimes, so Abe told me to slide under the door and unlock it. My head barely fit under the door, but I made it though. The strange stares received told us this wasn't common practice, but we did what we had to do.

So many people came up to us trying to sell us things. We did not understand English and were scared of being robbed. We focused on avoiding anyone who tried to approach us, while finding our way to the plane that was supposed to take us to our new home in Indiana. Our next flight was on Allegheny

Airlines and, after much searching, we finally located their ticket counter. Without knowing any English, it was only by some miracle that we managed to get our boarding passes. We found the right gate and were certain we were home free; however, we had no idea what was in store for us!

Neither Abe nor I realized that we needed to change planes two more times before arriving in Evansville. If the announcements were about changing planes, we had no idea since we could not understand what was said. We dutifully remained seated through each takeoff and landing, confident that our final stop would be Evansville. We were so wrong!

The cleaning crew was nearly done when they saw us sitting there. Two young kids looking frightened and confused with no idea what was happening. They kept talking to us, until it became apparent that neither of us understood a single word. After looking at our tickets, they must have realized that we were definitely in the wrong city. After a lot of chatter between them, one man came over, motioned with his hand for us to get up, and started leading us off the plane. Abe and I were filled with fear. We had no idea where they were taking us. We had no way to tell them what had happened or to ask for help to get to Evansville. We followed the man to the ticket counter where a number of Allegheny employees were gathered. While they were all talking, they kept looking over at us.

It was after midnight and from what we could guess, the next flight to Evansville was at 10:00 a.m. Abe was scared and shaking. Trying to comfort him and myself, I said, "Don't be fearful." I was hoping we were in good hands since by now, everyone was smiling at us. As I comforted Abe, I began to cry. All of the fear and frustration that I was feeling suddenly came out. I wanted my parents there, so they could tell us what to do.

At that moment, a beautiful flight attendant came over and smiled at us. While most of the other crewmembers appeared to be laughing about what had happened, she decided to be our lifesaver. Her sweet face was the only thing that calmed me down and I considered her an angel. She coordinated the new flight arrangements, a place for us to stay the night, and the transportation that would get us to the hotel and back to the airport in the morning. I had never met anyone who would go so far out of their way to help two strangers. It was not until later in life that I realized that most Americans I have known possess these same qualities.

Not long after she stepped in to help, Abe and I were driven to a nice hotel where we were given a room for the night. In the morning, we were served breakfast and shuttled back to the airport in time for the first flight. All of this was at no cost. We experienced for the first time outstanding customer service, a philosophy well-respected in this great nation.

Meanwhile, Reza, crazy with worry, waited for us to arrive in Indiana. Since there was no internet or cell phones yet, and answering machines were still rare, we had not been able to let him know what had happened. Reza had no idea where we were; he just knew that we were lost in the U.S.A.

After flying around the States for most of the day, we finally landed in Evansville. Reza had tears of joy as he greeted us. Finally, all of us could relax now that Abe and I were safely in Indiana. After some hugs, sharing the tales of our adventure, and some laughter, we loaded our suitcases into the car and headed toward our new home.

As we drove to Reza's apartment, Abe and I were stunned by how nice everything looked. The streets were clean and well kept. We passed children playing, and I saw parents with their kids walking down the street. Already, I missed my family tremendously. I did not know how I could get through this without them. So many thoughts and feelings raced through my mind as we made our way to our new home. My biggest fear was of the unknown … the new life we were beginning in America.

Once we arrived at our new home, we were greeted by Reza's roommate and then a few other people as they stopped by that evening. Being several years younger than everyone else, I felt very out of place. I greatly missed my parents and the rest of my family. There were times I felt so homesick and other times I felt completely empty inside. As the first few days passed, I did my best to settle into my new life, while Reza and Abe tried to comfort me.

It was December and the holiday season was in full swing with Christmas just around the corner. This made for a good distraction. We all enjoyed the spirit of the season in a beautiful church. Reza and his friends saw how much I missed my home and family, so they tried to cheer me up. We went on tours to see the holiday lights and glorious decorations. The holiday decorations, Christmas gatherings, and New Year's Eve celebrations were all new to me—and I was very impressed. The most amazing experience was seeing people kiss in public on New Year's Eve, when the countdown reached midnight and we rolled into 1979. Until then, I had never seen that type of public display. I was shocked when a woman I did not know ran up, kissed me, and wished me Happy New Year! Later, I learned that a midnight kiss on New

Year's Eve was a long-standing tradition and quite acceptable. Reza and his friends had a great time honoring this tradition and kissed many girls that fine New Year's Eve.

As the holidays came to a close, I knew the real world was out there waiting for me. The New Year had begun and my new life had begun as well. I enrolled at William Henry Harrison, the local high school, and prepared to start classes the first week in January 1979. The day before school started and not knowing what to expect was the scariest feeling. Everything was happening so quickly that many changes happened since we arrived.

I came to the States with only two suitcases filled with clothes, a few keepsakes, and enough money to pay for my living expenses and the cost of school for one year. That cash was a valuable asset that provided me a place to live, food to eat, and some other necessities in life. But money was definitely not the only thing of value that my father gave me. As I prepared to leave, my father told me three things:

▲ Appreciate every opportunity in life.

▲ Always respect everyone.

▲ Never compare yourself to anyone else.

Certainly, the money helped me survive. However, it was much later before I realized that my success in life came from putting the advice my father gave me into practice. I still follow those simple concepts every day.

2
NEW LIFE IN USA

I tried not to focus on how my entire world had turned upside down. I was suddenly living a new life in a strange world. My brothers were the only people I could communicate with and the only people I felt I could trust. I was homesick, missing my family, and the life I had before.

Few people could understand the fear I felt as I walked through the doors of an American school for the first time. I was stunned when I saw boys and girls holding hands, sixteen-year-old kids driving their own cars to school, and the disrespect sometimes shown to a teacher. The entire culture was completely unfamiliar to me. I was lost and afraid and even if I had wanted to tell someone, I only knew a few words in English. Not understanding what was being said to me was awkward, and I felt stupid for not knowing what was happening around me.

I managed to find my way around school and made it to all of my classes. I probably looked like every other student, but I really had no idea what was going on. I worked hard, but I still failed all of my classes that first semester. The principal gave me a note to take home requesting a parent/teacher conference. I handed the note to Reza, and since he was my legal guardian, he made an appointment to meet the principal.

As we entered the office, the principal looked at me and then looked at Reza, a typical 18-year-old, and shock and confusion came across his face. Once Reza explained why he was there, the principal's face softened. Then, he jokingly told Reza, "That is why this young boy is failing!" We all laughed, although I had no idea what was so funny. By the time we left, I understood that I had to turn things around in school or I faced being expelled for failing my classes.

It was hard to deal with feeling like a failure and part of me really wanted to give up. I was ashamed that I was doing so poorly and I didn't want the other kids to make fun of me. I felt like an outcast and that made me even more determined to find a way to turn my grades around. Those early years in school taught me that I needed to make some hard choices now. My parents sent me here so I would have a better life filled with more opportunities, and that started with me taking advantage of my education. If I was to reach the goal of a higher education and getting a college degree, I had to learn English well. So, that became my priority.

I became more determined than ever to focus on my studies and show my parents how much I appreciated the opportunity they made possible. Like many people who come to this great country, I was here to pursue "The American Dream."

Many kids at my school were not receptive to having a foreigner in their circle. They called me names and seemed to enjoy hurting me with their words and sometimes even physically. I tried to act strong and not let anyone see how much it hurt me, but at times it was more than I could handle. I would get angry or sad and want to strike out at them, but even then I knew that retaliation was not the answer.

I later realized that the way they treated me was not really about me. For some people, the only way they can feel powerful in life is by being a bully and try to take power from those around them. The students that gave me a hard time and tried to make me feel bad were the ones who felt bad about themselves. However, a few of my fellow students saw past our differences and were kind to me. Those students treated me with so much respect, and without prejudice or hate. They made an effort to help me when I needed it most.

One student, Linda, took the time to write down the definition of every word that I did not understand. She explained each word in detail so I was clear on their meaning. Her support was an important part of my success. To this day, I am grateful for the effort and encouragement I received from her and other students such as Chip, Patrick, and Debbie at Harrison. They made a huge impact on my life. When they would call or come over to give me a ride, I felt cared for. They included me in their circle and I can't thank them enough for that gift of encouragement. I think about how many people have helped me over the years and pay it forward whenever I can offer encouragement and support to another.

My first couple of semesters attending high school in America were extremely challenging. I learned English, in addition to my regular classes, and I dealt with kids making fun of me, insulting me, and beating me for no other reason than I was different from them. At times, I became depressed and thought my life would never get any better so I should give up. Over time though, I began surrounding myself with classmates who were friendly and accepting. I became good friends with several kids and having them cheer me on helped change my attitude. I told myself to stay strong, spend time with positive people, and keep working hard toward reaching my dreams.

My priority was to learn English as quickly as possible, even though I could not write or speak it when I first arrived, and I still had to keep up with all of my classes. I began carrying a dictionary with me wherever I went. When someone used a word that I did not know, I would ask him or her to spell out that word so I could look up the definition. It helped me greatly to learn the definition and understand the conversion, but as you might imagine, some people would become frustrated when I interrupted them, asked them to spell out a word, and then they waited while I looked up the word and read its definition. I knew that it was the best and fastest way to learn English.

My first semester, different subjects intimidated me. With everything in English, the lessons made no sense to me. However, once I had a plan to learn English and acted on it, I was no longer afraid. Even though I had failed all of my classes that first semester, I realized the language barrier caused it. So, I decided to change the situation and eliminate the barrier. I did not give up. I asked my teachers for help, too. I was surprised how my history teacher, Mr. Washington, put in extra time and effort. He created special projects that allowed me to earn extra credit, so I could pass his class. He helped me succeed, and he showed me that I mattered.

While not perfect, my plan to learn English paid off. I caught on quickly and understood a great deal more of written and spoken English. This helped me concentrate on my schoolwork and I passed every class the following semester. In doing so, I put an end to my fear of failure. From that victory, I realized the importance of creating a plan and acting on it. Many times, you will find that the only difference between success and failure is whether or not you make a plan to reach your goal and take action.

Even though Abe and I had just settled in to life in Evansville, things were about to change. Reza announced that he wanted to attend college in Ohio. At first, I wanted Abe and I to remain in Indiana until I finished high school. Abe found living in America and being away from his wife too difficult and wanted to move back to Iran to be with her. So after approximately two months in America, Abe flew back to Iran. This meant that Reza and I would move from Indiana to Ohio, so that he could attend Ohio State University.

Reza and I packed up what little we had and headed for Columbus. Luckily, we had some friends in Ohio who we knew from childhood, which made our transition to yet another place a little easier. I continued high school while Reza continued college.

The road became extremely bumpy when the war broke out in Iran and continued fighting put an end to any possibility of seeing our family anytime soon—if at all. As the war began to spread, I grew increasingly worried that I would never see my family again. One day, after watching some news coverage of the war back home, fear and sadness overcame me. I felt that if I didn't move back to Iran right then, I would never see my family again.

Although Reza tried to persuade me to stay, the next day, I bought my ticket for a flight home and packed my bags. He could see that I was determined and finally helped by arranging for me to stay with his friends in New York during the overnight stop for my return flight. Saying goodbye to Reza and the friends that I had made was hard, but I was so afraid for my family.

As I sat on the first leg of my flight home, thoughts of all I was giving up plagued me. Did I waste all the time and effort I had put into succeeding since I arrived in the U.S.A.? I realized my struggle between the future and the past, and knew that if I stayed here, many sacrifices were needed. Not seeing my family anytime soon, and with no financial help, there was the challenge of surviving with little food and a place to stay. To avoid homelessness, cutting spending on all levels was necessary.

My father found out that I was on a plane headed back to Iran, and insisted that Reza stop me before I boarded my final flight home the following day. The war escalated and my father knew that as soon as I arrived, I'd be forced to join the military and immediately sent to fight along the front lines, unlike Abe who had no legal obligation to fight since he was married and expecting a child. Not only would the government prevent me from seeing my family, I likely would have been killed in a senseless war.

Before my plane landed in New York, Reza had arranged with his friends to have me call him as soon as I arrived. As I walked off the plane, I already began wondering if I made the right decision. Reza's friends picked me up at the airport and they told me on the drive to their home that I was to call Reza as soon as possible. I wondered why he needed to speak with me so urgently, and anxiously dialed our home phone once we arrived at his friends' house.

Reza told me that he called our parents and our father said to tell me, "You must stay in the U.S.A. and pursue your dreams." He went on to tell me what would happen if I boarded that plane the following day. I spent almost the entire night thinking about everything. I realized that giving up everything and flying home was not a good decision. In fact, it probably would have resulted in my death.

My longing for family and my insecurities about my future and that of my family had clouded my thinking. The only wise choice was for me to stay in America, continue pursuing my dreams by working hard and living up to my potential. I never regretted not returning to Iran, even though it meant I would not see my family again until nine years later.

Once I returned safely to Ohio, I remembered the enormous sacrifices I had to make if I wanted to stay in the United States. I thought that living without my parents in the U.S. was temporary. I'd attend school here, but sooner or later, I'd return to my parents' home and to the life I once knew. I realized the truth that there was no going back. I could only keep moving forward and working toward accomplishing my goals. I knew that doing so without the daily support of my family wouldn't be easy.

Seeing what my fear and insecurity had almost caused me to do, I no longer feared my future in America. Although uncertain of what field to pursue, I knew that I wanted to continue my education after high school. Seeing people working as professionals, living in a nice home, and having financial freedom, gave me the drive to reach that dream myself.

I started by setting goals for my future. Some goals I could achieve in the near future, within a few months. Others would take a year or longer to achieve. Regardless of the time it took, I knew the importance of me staying positive and to keep working toward making them happen.

The first goal I set was to gain more independence by getting my driver's license when I turned 16. This was an exciting opportunity for me that was truly a dream come true. First, I learned the traffic laws, and prepared to take the written test for my learner's permit. I had actually learned how to drive very early in life. Children drove much younger where I grew up and I was always passionate about cars. Passing the driving test should be easy; however, the written exam challenged me. So, I studied the driving laws every day until test time.

After failing on my first go around, I passed the written portion on my second try. I was ready to take the driving portion, and take on the world, but I needed to wait until I turned 16 and had the required number of hours behind the wheel. I drove Reza's Ford Mustang every chance I could until I believed Reza was tired of never getting to drive his own car.

Eventually, I turned 16 and took the driving test to get my license. I'll never forget the look on the examiner's face as I parallel parked perfectly without hesitation. He said "Son, where did you learn how to drive?"

I said, "Just years of experience, sir," which made him laugh so hard, he nearly forgot to mark my test as passing. It felt great to reach my first goal and it increased my confidence in what I could do in the future.

Reza was happy and worried at the same time when it came to me having a driver's license. I still insisted on driving him everywhere we went together. Eventually, he adjusted and actually sat in the back seat with his girlfriend whenever we went places. He had found his personal chauffeur, and I was happy to be of service.

My next goal was to purchase my own car, but I did not have the finances to do so right away. We kept sharing a car until I had saved enough money to buy my own, which took me about year or so. I bought a beautiful VW Golf, and Reza owned a Chevy Monte Carlo after trading in his Mustang. We were both happy that we no longer had to share a car.

Sadly, this happiness was short-lived when we hit a bumpy financial situation and Reza ended up selling his car. Then, I had let Reza borrow my car to travel to New York for a possible job opportunity. The first evening he was in New York, my supervisor came to me during my shift saying that I had an emergency phone call. Reza frantically said my car had been stolen.

At first, panic washed over me, since we no longer had a way for either of us to get to work and school. He was very upset, and now greatly regretted selling his car. To make matters worse, my car only had liability insurance, which put us at ground zero again. After we hung up, I took a deep breath, and decided the best way to deal with it was to concentrate on my job. I immediately offered to work more hours and my boss was grateful to have the help. I knew that the more I worked, the faster we could save money, and the faster we could buy another car.

The very evening after Reza came back from New York, I was at home relaxing from a long day at work when I heard this loud explosion outside of our apartment window. I quickly ran out to see what was going on. In the parking lot, I saw Reza getting out of this ugly blue 1972 VW Bug, with its rear fender missing from an accident. The muffler, also gone, sounded like a tank, and it backfired loudly whenever he turned it off. It was embarrassing. That aside, the car had no heater, making it unsafe to drive in the winter. I asked Reza why he bought this piece of junk and he said $700 was all he had to buy the beauty.

I knew that I had to save up money fast as this "beauty" was not going to handle taking me to work and Reza to school for very long, especially with winter setting in. The car was so loud that we were stopped almost daily by the police. There was no fender so there was no tail light. I would explain that we didn't have the money to get it fixed, so most times we would get away with a warning, but once we were given a ticket that cost approximately $60.

A friend had a white VW Bug with a nice body, but it had no transmission. So we took the transmission from our car and put it into his Bug. It was a summer project for us that worked. We used that car for quite a while.

Before the Bug was finished, I tried to get another car as soon as possible, I saved $375 within a month and purchased a well-maintained 1972 Oldsmobile Delta88. The car ran very well and looked just as good. The only problem was it had some rust holes on the floorboards. I had visions of driving like Fred Flintstone. Whenever it would rain, water would get inside the car and trunk.

Even with these problems, we felt our transportation problems were solved, and we were optimistic about the future. We had overcome another setback, so Reza continued working on his college degree to become an electrical engineer. I continued working with the firm belief that I would someday finish my college education and land a professional job.

When reflecting on these experiences, I can't believe that was us, but indeed it was! We did not give up when faced with obstacles, and once we worked through them, we began rebuilding right away. We relentlessly pursued our dreams and they became reality over the years.

When it came to earning a living, I never turned down a job opportunity and worked a number of different jobs. To make ends meet, I was a server at a restaurant, a valet, and even worked sales at Victoria's Secret. Selling women's lingerie was never a goal of mine, but finding an honest way to make money was my focus.

My longest employment was at a major chain hotel, which was unionized. At first, I did not understand the purpose of the union, but later I realized how the union saved people from being mistreated by unreasonable employers. I was glad to know the union was behind me and would protect me from discrimination and harassment. I considered the union to be one of my biggest breaks from those days because it enabled me to continue my employment and saved me from the ugliness certain supervisors imposed on the employees. Those years, I worked as a valet cashier and driver, busboy, and room service waiter. These were not planned occupations, but I learned a lot from each job.

The years from 1978 to 1988 were the most critical and challenging years of my life. These years laid the foundation for who I am as an individual—one who survived much just to be able to stay in this great country. I learned from many people along the way, and every experience during this time was an opportunity to add to my wisdom and common sense.

I continued taking classes, working toward my bachelor's degree. I knew that a four-year college degree increased the opportunities I would have to enter the professional arena and obtain a higher paying job. With all of the financial challenges, I sought alternative ways to pay for college including grants and student loans. Between tuition, books, and living expenses, life was expensive and keeping my head above water could be difficult at times.

Along the way, there were many bad influences trying to motivate me with false promises to wander off my path and do wrong things to earn big money. I resisted those temptations by recalling the simple lessons my parents had taught me which were about "being good" and "doing good." Earning an honest living, regardless of how tough it may be, will eventually pay off in a big way.

I worked relentlessly during that time, taking on as many shifts as I could to save money to pay for my education and future expenses. I attended college full time and worked full time in order to put myself through school. I finally graduated with my bachelor's degree and started on my career in 1988.

My first goal after college was to get a professional job. I wanted that job so I could reach my next two goals of buying a Honda Civic and a two-bedroom house. When I first set my sights on those goals, I had no idea how I would make them happen, but with hard work I knew I would. Achieving each of those dreams made me proud and very happy.

Being so far away from my family and in a completely different environment could have made it easy for me to become involved with the wrong people and to make decisions that did not support my goals or help me to succeed. Fortunately, I recognized this early on, so I knew it was up to me to find ways to stay on my chosen path.

I started by writing down the words of wisdom and positive ideas that my parents and other loved ones had shared with me. I would repeat them to myself. I also started keeping a journal of my thoughts and asked those people who I knew cared most about me to share their thoughts, as well.

Any time I would be tempted by someone or something that would not help me reach my goals, I would remember the good advice and read from my journal. If I was confused, I knew my trusted friends would offer answers or advice that was best for me. One of my closest friends always said, "It is so hard to be good, but very easy to be bad."

Many would probably agree that temptations and bad influences are everywhere. Making choices without thinking about the consequences, may cause pain in one's life. It isn't that people can't have fun, only that it is important to walk within the lines while having fun.

There were times during my teenage and adolescent years when I was tempted to do things with my friends that were outrageous or even illegal; however, I stayed focused on the future and knew that I wanted my dreams to become true, instead of turning into a nightmare.

Looking back at my first years in America, I realize that initially, I was driven by fear. One day though, I woke up and knew that if I worked hard and stayed focused, everything would work out well. I began reminding myself of the words my father always taught me. "Do not be fearful. As long as you have good intentions in life, everything will work out."

Overcoming fear of doing things is not easy for most

people. While I share about how I did it and make it sound simple, in truth, fear is real. One important fact that helped me was changing my perception of it. *I learned that I will not be any worse off if I try to overcome fear and fail, but I will be much better off if I try to overcome fear and succeed.*

The concept of not fearing took hold of me then. It became one of the main reasons for my survival and my success in life—even to this day. I take chances to improve my life and make a positive impact on those around me.

I chose to pursue the American Dream, and worked to reach every positive goal possible without being afraid of failure along the way. I knew another important key in achieving my dreams was to "work hard and play smart." I did this by focusing on my studies, making smart choices, and surrounding myself with people who live their lives with honesty and integrity in all that they do.

3

COMING OF AGE

Much like a roller coaster ride, my first three years in the U.S. were filled with many ups and downs. It sometimes felt as if life hit me with one challenge after another. Filled with doubt, I wondered if I could make it through, but I knew that I had to keep moving forward.

Once I decided what I wanted for my future and kept those goals in the forefront of my mind, the way I experienced life began to change. Notice that I did not say that my life changed and that is because life did not change—I did. There were still setbacks and challenges, and things did not always go my way. However, by focusing on my goals and knowing that with hard work I could achieve them, my attitude and my reactions changed.

Whether I wanted to see my family so badly that I ached inside, faced another financial struggle, or missed an opportunity that would have benefited me in some way, I had come to understand that feelings of fear, disappointment, frustration, and sadness were only temporary. In reality, any obstacle in my path was rarely as insurmountable as I imagined, if I let those negative feelings take over my mind. Although I still missed my family a great deal, my mind no longer filled with thoughts of flying back to Iran whenever a problem arose. Deep down, I knew that regardless of what happened today, there was always tomorrow. And tomorrow was another opportunity for me to succeed.

As my senior year wore on, I was very busy studying and working to save money for college. I was both nervous and excited about graduating high school and attending college. My first day of high school in Indiana frightened me, but now I comfortably attended classes, walked the halls, and definitely fit in. Soon, I would proudly receive my diploma and then start school over again, but this time at an institution of higher education.

Almost everything my parents had told me about why they were sending me to live in the U.S. had to do with the opportunities available to me by earning a college degree. What I had experienced since moving to the U.S. also confirmed the importance of having a college degree.

With the help of my school counselor, Reza, and a few supportive friends, I began researching colleges and applying for any financial aid I could find—educational grants, scholarships, and student loans, etc.; anything that would help me cover the cost of tuition and books. Once again, I knew that now I lived in the greatest country in the world, one with opportunities beyond my wildest imagination.

Without the benefit of financial aid, attending college

for my bachelor's degree was going to be challenging. It would take me at least an additional year or two to graduate. I could only attend college part-time, since I would be working more to pay for it. I would anxiously check the mail each day, hoping to receive a congratulatory letter for even just one of the countless financial aid applications I had submitted.

Finally, after several disappointments, I received notice of my first award. It was enough to cover some of my tuition and I would receive the same amount all four years. To me, it was confirmation that anyone with a strong work ethic who will pursue relentlessly the many opportunities available to all can undoubtedly achieve the American Dream.

Other award letters came too, for scholarships and grants that altogether made it possible for me to attend college full-time, although I decided to still work full-time, as well. Ultimately, I chose to stay in Columbus and attend Franklin University. Once I received my acceptance letter from Franklin, I was eager to jump into college life.

As I finished high school and prepared to start college, Reza received his degree, along with a job offer in New York. He packed up and headed off to live on Long Island, launching his career and furthering his search for the American Dream. We each had taken our own path on our journey, but have always kept in touch along the way.

When I look back on my college years, I realize that without maintaining a positive attitude, I probably would have given up. I could have quit school and worked full-time, however, I was certain that taking the easy way out was not going to help me reach my goals. Instead, I was up every morning at 6:00 a.m. to study and still made it to class by 8:00 a.m. During the winter months, I prayed every morning that my car would start, so I could arrive at school on time. Walking to the car, warming up the engine, deicing the windows usually took 30 minutes, which tortured me.

After attending six hours of classes, I finished at 2:00 p.m. and had barely an hour to eat and study some more before having to arrive at work by 3:00 p.m. to start my 8-hour shift. By the time I was off at 11:00 p.m., I faced another round of warming the car and deicing the windows. Since it was coldest at night, half of the time I would have to pull out my jumper cables and rely on the kindness of strangers to help me start my car. I have never tolerated freezing weather well, so I set a goal to relocate to a milder climate after I finished college, another piece of the puzzle to my American Dream.

Regardless of how difficult and demanding my schedule could be, my optimistic outlook rarely wavered. If I did have a moment of feeling tired or down, I knew that it was normal and certainly understandable, given my circumstances. When I returned home, I would take a few minutes and write down my thoughts and feelings. Then, I would read what I wrote and adjust my perspective to regain my optimism and redirect my focus to my goal.

For example, when frustrated about the bitter cold, I accepted that I do not like cold weather. Also, I'd remind myself that cold weather will pass and my being cold is temporary, too. I might also note how long it will be before the weather starts to warm up. It was at a time just as I'm describing when I decided that living in a warmer climate was an important goal. Lastly, I would often remember how far I have come and how grateful I am for everything I do have and all of the help I have received. It was hard for me to stay unhappy or down when I shifted my mindset to gratitude.

No matter how I was feeling, I always treated those around me with the highest level of respect and never took my frustrations out on others. Directing bitterness or anger toward other people only leads to hurt feelings, damaged relationships and closed lines of communication.

If I noticed that a friend, a fellow student, or a co-worker was feeling down, I would offer a friendly ear or an encouraging word—something I still do today. Oftentimes, the smallest sincere gesture I gave to people made a big impact and helped them feel better.

Even though I had little time during college, I did try to help others whenever I could. Years later, I'm now very busy with my family, a career as a healthcare executive, and other business dealings, yet I still make time to offer my assistance whenever the opportunity presents itself and I am happier for it.

For my first three years at Franklin, my schedule was consistent. Working and going to school full-time required a great deal of discipline and some sacrifices too, but I knew that to achieve my goals in life, it was more than worth it.

At the start of my senior year, I was offered a position in business development with a startup computer company. This was the early 80s and the tech industry was nothing like it is today. The PC led the way and small businesses would buy top of the line turnkey computer systems that came with a 20MB hard drive, a monochrome monitor, and a floppy disk drive.

After considering the opportunity and assessing the risk, I decided to accept the position even though the industry itself was still in its infancy. Having limited knowledge of computers and no experience selling them, there were many uncertainties and I had many concerns. I was grateful for the opportunity though, so I focused on the possibilities with this new venture and did not let my fear stop me from trying.

I took pride in my work and genuinely cared about my customers—working hard to help businesses understand how a computerized business management system could meet their needs. Providing excellent customer service has always been important to me, and it was critical at this time. Since most people were not yet familiar with computers and did not understand the true value of owning or using one, I had a number of solid objections to overcome when talking with potential customers.

The company painted a beautiful picture about the potential of the business and promised me the world—once I delivered results. I was very optimistic about my future with the company, so I developed a great marketing strategy and worked relentlessly to exceed their expectations.

Unfortunately, one thing that I did not do was to have management put everything we agreed to in writing. My word is my bond and at that time, it did not occur to me that people in business operated any other way. When it came time, I went back to management expecting them to make good on all they had promised, but instead they denied ever agreeing to our original terms. Other than my regular pay, I did not benefit from the company's success, as promised, and now I was unemployed.

It was a big disappointment and hard for me to accept being treated unfairly. After I had time to think about it, I realized that although it was difficult, it was a valuable life lesson. The experience taught me to be cautious in business dealings and to get everything in writing. I looked at this as a minor setback and set out to find a new job.

The computer industry grew and I was confident of quickly landing another job. In between classes, I would daily check the help-wanted ads and drop off my résumé to nearby companies in hopes of speaking with the person who did the hiring. Although I had worked for a short time selling computers, I was told repeatedly that I did not have enough experience. Hearing this frustrated me at times, but I reminded myself that I was capable of the tasks required and kept my sights set on finding gainful employment so I could show it.

I remember giving myself a day to work through the disappointment and sadness of being unemployed. Once that day ended, I started making a new plan to find work and achieve my goals. By now, I was close to finishing my degree and once I did, I was free to leave Columbus. I continued to look for work in my field and expanded the search area, since I would be able to relocate soon.

Because I had financial obligations, I took a job back in the food and beverage industry to pay my bills. I could have easily considered doing so a failure and let that belief eat away at my self-confidence. However, I realized that the road to achieving my goals, like any other road, could contain twists and turns.

4

REUNITING

My parents were coming to America!

Out of the blue, Reza called me. He was yelling into the phone and talking so fast that I couldn't make out what he was saying. Once he calmed down, I finally understood why he was so excited. Our parents would be arriving in San Francisco the next day!

I am uncertain that there are strong enough words to describe the emotions I felt the day that I left for America. Even now, when I think back to that long car ride to the airport, what stands out most was how tightly my mother held my hand the entire way. With an endless stream of tears staining her cheeks, she gripped my hand as if I was dangling from the side of a cliff and she was the only one who could save me. Overwhelmed with my own nervousness and fear about what I was facing and how I would survive, I also hung on for dear life.

Saying our goodbyes at the airport was more than any of us could bear. Everyone sobbed and held one another when my mother began pleading with my father to change our plans and not let us go. My father held her hand and looked deeply into her eyes. Then, he slowly shook his head as he wiped away her tears. My mother stopped asking and simply nodded. She knew that no matter how heartbreaking it was to send her sons so far away, it was far more important to give us the opportunity to have better lives.

I had no idea how I would cope with not seeing my mother, father, sisters, or grandparents. The distance between my family and me was very apparent as soon as our plane took flight. Soon, our parents were a world apart from us, and as the days passed, feelings of emptiness overcame me.

We were always close to our aunts, uncles, nieces, and cousins, too. Growing up, I was surrounded by a loving and supportive family—one that I could turn to for anything. Now, other than Abe and Reza, who were still very young themselves, there was no one in America to guide me and help me adjust to this new world. Life became very difficult.

The distance between my family and me felt infinite from the moment our plane touched down. Our family was a world away from us and as the days passed, feelings of emptiness washed over me. Many times, I wanted to tell my mother goodnight, ask for my father's guidance, or tell my family about a new experience that I had, but because of the high cost of international phone calls, the most we could do was to write to one another. Young people today often find it hard to believe, but in those days, home phones and the postal service were the only way for people to stay in touch.

When I left for America, my mother and I had agreed

that we would write one another at least twice a week. I asked her to keep me updated on all of our family and to include a familiar recipe in every letter. Knowing what was happening with my family helped me to feel a part of their lives. Starting a collection of family recipes helped me to learn to cook. Eating fast food was exciting and different at first, but eventually, I grew tired of it and I missed the dishes my mother served our family. Cooking these meals for myself and enjoying the smells and tastes of home, would bring me great comfort, and as a bonus, I became a good cook!

The bond between my family and me played an important role in helping me to stay the course in life. The love we shared was always strong and because of that, I made choices that demonstrated honor and respect for them. It was important to make my family proud and to not disappoint them.

Fortunately, I grew up in a very open and expressive family. Our bond was solid well before I left for the U.S. and withstood the test of distance for years through letter writing and the occasional phone call. Early in our written exchanges, I received many tear-stained letters from my mother filled with news of my family and friends. Often times, the news we shared was outdated by the time the letters arrived, but it was still so important to all of us to keep connected as best we could.

It was difficult finding out that I lost my cousin and a close friend in the war, and even more heartbreaking losing my grandparents, aunt, and uncle without being able to say goodbye or be there to grieve with my family. I came to realize that loss was a part of life and I had to accept it and keep moving forward.

No matter how many or how often we exchanged letters, the fear of not seeing my parents again was always present. Looking back, I know my mother and father made a huge sacrifice having three of their sons travel thousands of miles away with no way to guarantee our safety or success. Each of us grew up missing our parents and kept moving forward with the hope of seeing them again one day.

Nine years of forced separation had passed when without notice, our parents had the chance to visit America. Concerned that they might be prohibited from leaving Iran, my parents did not purchase their tickets until they had received their visas and were ready to immediately board a plane. They told no one that they were even thinking about taking a trip.

But there was a problem. Although Reza was now living in Northern California, he was out of town on business and could not return home for several days. Since I was still living in Ohio, neither of us would be able to meet our parents at the airport!

After years of praying for and envisioning the moment we would all be reunited, Reza and I could not even greet our mother and father when they arrived in the States! Moreover, they knew no one and would have no idea where to go or what to do. Reza and I were sick with worry, but we agreed to remain optimistic knowing that we would figure out a solution.

As I brainstormed for ideas by talking with my friends, one of them reminded me that our friend, Jimmy, had moved out to California a few years prior—and settled in, of all places, San Francisco. The very place my parents were landing in twenty-four hours. After furiously searching my papers, I found Jimmy's phone number and quickly dialed the number.

Thankfully, he answered on the first try and I frantically began explaining our dilemma.

Jimmy interrupted my anxious pleas for help by stating that he would be happy to greet my parents at the San Francisco Airport, drive them to his home, and host them until my brother or I arrived. Jimmy's willingness to help and his words of comfort filled me with a sense of calm. He asked for a description of my mother and father and continued to reassure me that he would handle everything and that would be fine.

That is when I realized how important it is to always surround myself with positive and supportive friends and to invest in my relationships with them. Even when I first moved to the U.S. and was barely able to communicate with those around me, I could recognize people who were genuine and who had the best of intentions. Those were the people I wanted in my life. I'm still close with some of them to this day.

Now that I could let Reza know that our parents would be helped once they landed, I immediately turned my attention to getting to San Francisco as quickly as possible. Flying there was out of the question since same day ticket prices were outrageous and I knew a bus or train would take too long. So, I threw a few necessities into my suitcase and jumped in my car and hit the road. I was excited and overjoyed knowing I would finally be reunited with my parents. After years of wishing and worrying, it was finally going to come true.

It is over 2,500 miles from Columbus to San Francisco and I drove it in three days straight, stopping only to fillup my gas tank, stretch a little, and grab something to eat on the road. I wasn't worried about the drive, the car, or the cost. All

I cared about was getting there and seeing my mother and father for the first time in nine years.

Once I was on the road, I remembered what happened to Abe and me when we arrived in the U.S. and how frightened we both were. I wondered what would become of my parents should they get lost or end up arriving with no one to meet them and my mind would start to race. I would begin to panic, but then I would hear my friend's voice calmly telling me not to worry, he would take care of my folks, and they would be safe. Knowing Jimmy was there for my parents and replaying his words in my head helped me overcome my fears and stay optimistic. Knowing he was there for me allowed me to focus on getting there safely.

When I was about halfway to San Francisco, I called Jimmy from a gas station pay phone to find out if my parents had arrived. I could not believe how relieved I was to hear that they were in San Francisco and everything had gone fine. Well, almost everything. My mother and father were shocked and somewhat concerned when they were unexpectedly greeted at the airport by a stranger. They were reluctant to go with Jimmy at first, but once they understood why Reza and I were not there to meet them and that we would be there soon, they agreed to leave the airport with him. Jimmy had driven them to a motel, helped them get a room, and made certain they had everything they needed for the moment. I told Jimmy how grateful I was for his help until Reza or I arrived and he assured me he would keep an eye on them until then.

Until the moment Jimmy explained what had happened, my mother and father had been looking for Reza and me, expecting all of us to finally be together again after being apart for far too long. Many times over the years, I had dreamt of my parents visiting America and us finally being reunited. I imagined what it would be like seeing them at the airport— happy hearts, loving hugs, tears of joy. I never envisioned anything even close to what actually happened and I felt bad for my parents, but there was nothing any of us could do to make it different.

Once I knew my parents were in California, it was more real to me and my excitement continued to build. Not being with them felt like a waste of precious time and I kept driving as fast as I could. My mind filled with so many questions. How would they react to seeing me as a young man for the first time? I didn't have the money for a camera or processing photos, so they hadn't seen me. What did they look like after so many years? What would they think of America? What would they think of me?

Once I finally crossed into California and stopped to fill-up, I called Reza's home to get directions. I heard my mother's screams of joy in the background once she realized Reza was talking with me. I was exhausted, yet energized at the thought of being so close and had to ask Reza to repeat the directions to his home several times. The last hour on the road felt like an eternity.

Before I could take my finger off the doorbell, Reza's front door opened and I saw my parents' faces after almost a decade of being apart. My mother ran to me crying and squeezed me harder than I have ever been held by anyone. Finally, Reza and my father guided us into the house, still clinging to one another. Once inside, my parents sandwiched me in a bear hug and tears flowed for all of us. Years of being apart, of sadness and longing, and of fear had finally come to an end.

Although I had always known it, my mother told me

how hard it had been to send her youngest child thousands of miles away from home when he was only fourteen. Now she was stunned to see me standing before her—a man at twenty-three! She told me it was very bittersweet. She was proud of the man she saw now and sad at having missed out on being there while I grew up. As much as Reza and I missed our parents, we were always focused on surviving, building our lives, and making our American Dreams come true. I think the years had passed more slowly for my parents.

I cannot imagine the day-to-day worry they must have felt wondering if I was all right. They were good parents. The few times we communicated brought reassurance to them, but it must have been hard for them.

The reuniting visit helped us reconnect as a family giving opportunity to celebrate the fruition of my time here. We enjoyed a couple of weeks together with my family seeing the northern California landscape (San Francisco, Santa Cruz, San Jose) and driving down the Pacific Coast Highway (PCH), then cross country back to Ohio. They only stayed less than a month in the U.S.A. The time went quickly.

I did not want to say good bye to my parents again, but I had to return to my life in Ohio. Since they were able to stay longer, wanted to experience America, and wanted to spend more time with me, they asked to accompany me on the drive back to Columbus. The trip turned out to be one of the most memorable events of my life. A joy-filled eight days alone with my parents that I did not want to end.

We headed south from San Francisco along the PCH— one of the most beautiful coastal drives in America. We stopped often on the way to Los Angeles to capture the majesty of the most breathtaking scenery ever. I remember my father saying over and over, "Beautiful America is heaven on earth." Experiencing such magnificence was moving for each of us and we spent our time in the car sharing thoughts of gratitude, appreciation, and love.

In Strafford, Missouri, we went through the Wild Animal Safari, which is a drive-thru zoo. It fascinated us seeing all the animals loose from cages and walking around. Many animals came to our car looking for food. My dad thought it would be neat to feed an ostrich, so he rolled down his window and gave a snack to him from the car. Suddenly, two or three more ostriches stuck their necks in the car window. My dad was throwing everything from orange peels to brochures at the ostriches to get them out. My mother screamed from fear. I just sped up the car almost taking an ostrich head with me. I looked at my dad and with restraint said, "We cannot open the windows here." There were signs everywhere saying that and we found out it was true.

I will always be grateful for our road trip to Ohio. It was one of the greatest gifts I could ever receive. Not only do I still have wonderful memories, it also taught me the importance of being in the moment with those around you. Without the distractions of today's electronics, we remained completely engaged with one another—free from the pull of cell phones, mp3 players, tablets, etc.

My family and I put aside all of our electronics for a few minutes at least once a day. Except in rare instances, we turned off our phones and all other electronics at meal time and other times when we are all together throughout the day. It is the easiest way to encourage conversation and connection when we are together. We share our thoughts and experiences while everyone is present and listening.

The drive down the coast was the first of many wonderful memories from our adventure. Now that my parents have passed on, I look back and realize how spending quality time with them and sharing our love and appreciation for one another made a positive impact on the quality of my life. I am forever grateful for all the time I spent with my mother and father. I'm more thankful for the sacrifices they made to send me to America and for the opportunities it provided me.

5

NEWFOUND OPPORTUNITIES

Reuniting with my parents and being able to show them America was one of the highlights of my life. Spending time with my folks not only quieted the ache I felt at having been apart for nearly a decade, it also reenergized me. Their acceptance, support, and pride at my accomplishments and the young man that I had become renewed my determination.

It was nearing graduation and once they returned to Iran, I decided it was time to focus on the next chapter of my life—launching my career. This was still in the days before Google, before online job searches, and even before the Internet. I began my job hunt at my university's career center. The staff was happy to help me gain a clear understanding of possible career choices, assistance with my résumé and cover letter, and job hunting tips that helped me jumpstart my search. All of which proved to be invaluable now that I started down my career path.

While I had worked my way through high school and college, those jobs were simply a means to an end. I earned money to cover my expenses and pay my way through school. My goals were far greater in life, yet I knew that to reach them, I had to position myself on the path to success. The first step on that path was being able to support myself while continuing my education. These jobs rarely paid more than minimum wage and I knew I would move on once I had my degree and found work in my field. Still, I was grateful to be employed. I took pride in my work and understood that my employer and their customers relied on me to do the best job possible.

A strong work ethic is something I learned in childhood. As far back as I can remember, my parents told me to put forth my best effort in all that I do. You can find fulfillment and self-satisfaction in a job well done. Whether it is coursework, household chores, or job duties, it is a reflection of who you are. It forms people's opinion of you, shapes your future, and can greatly influence what opportunities come your way. Knowing this, I always committed to doing my best, even in those first few jobs, and I treated my job search the same way.

Once my résumé was done, I began applying for jobs in my field. Given the weather in Columbus, I was hoping to relocate, but I started my search with nearby companies. With all things being equal, a local job candidate would likely have an advantage over someone who needed to relocate and I wanted to keep my options open. Even if I was determined to relocate, getting a few professional interviews under my belt boosted my confidence and improved my interviewing skills.

Although I followed the career center's advice and rehearsed being interviewed, I still remember how anxious I became during my first couple of interviews.

I approached finding a job the same way I approached working a job. I gained a clear understanding of the job descriptions and types of companies that interested me. Then, I made a list of the tasks I needed to complete to find out about openings and apply for them. I blocked out time each day for my career search, so it became part of my routine. I made a habit of keeping detailed records of my job search, so I knew what jobs I had applied for, what I had submitted, and when I needed to follow up.

I also made a point of enlisting the help of others in my job search. Early on, all of my friends knew that I was searching for a full-time career position. However, I did not stop there. Whenever I met someone new, if the timing was right, I'd often ask people about their line of work. This easily led into me saying that I was about to graduate college and was looking for a job. I'd also ask the person about the job market in their field, or if they were from out of town, how the job market looked in their area. It surprised me how many people took an interest in the conversation and happily answered my questions. I learned about companies and job openings that I probably would never have found on my own.

Of course, if there was some way for me to benefit the other person, I would definitely do that too. While I did not know it at the time, I was networking—connecting with others to share resources and knowledge. Offering and asking for help can be a very valuable skill to benefit both people. When I started talking to others about my job search, I quickly realized that people enjoy sharing their story, and if they can, most people also enjoy helping others. Most people like helping others because it makes them feel good about themselves. Genuinely helping people without expectations is well-received and appreciated by them. They most likely will not forget your kindness to them.

In some ways, I look at my life as a garden made up of all the different experiences I've had. My actions and words are seeds that I scatter wherever I go. If I plant positive seeds and do so with care, I know that some of those seeds will sprout and flourish. In doing so, they can bring great things to my life both big and small—and often when I least expect it!

This was true of my first jobs too. These jobs were fine while I was working on finishing college; the companies worked with my school schedule and I could earn money for bills. However, these jobs were not in my field of study and I never thought about making a career out of any of them. Even so, I took each job seriously and made certain to do my best regardless of the task. I could have easily done just enough to get by, cut corners, or rushed through the work. After all, back then, there were plenty of part-time jobs and who would it hurt if I didn't do my best work?

During my sophomore year of college, I was working as a hotel valet. The work was easy, the tips were great, and getting to drive some of the exotic cars was exciting and always made for great bragging rights. While there, I made a number of friends, although some I had lost contact with once I left.

It was at the end of my senior year when I ran into Sam while stopping at a restaurant to grab a bite before my Monday evening class. When I first spotted him seated alone at a nearby table, it took me a couple of minutes to remember his name and how we had met. Sam had only been hired on as a valet a couple of months before I left, but he trained with me when he first started, so we had the chance to talk and had gotten to know one another.

I walked over to Sam's table, said hello, and reminded him of my name and where we had met, just in case he did not remember. He remembered me and was genuinely pleased to see me. I was ordering food to go and asked if I could join him while I waited. Once he said yes, I sat down across from him and asked him what he had been up to since I left the hotel. Sam was happy and doing well. He had completed EMT training and was working as a paramedic. Of course, when he asked about me, I told him that I would graduate in a couple of weeks and I was putting my time and energy into finding a full-time job.

Sam and I continued our conversation until the server dropped off my "to-go" order. As I was saying goodbye and getting up to leave, Sam asked if I remembered Marcus and Ben who had also worked as valets. I told him I did. He said that they had moved to Southern California to work for a startup technology firm, adding that he could see if there were more openings. I could not believe what I heard. I was so excited and had so many questions, but I needed to get to class. I had to borrow the server's pen to write down my phone number so Sam could let me know what he found out.

A couple of times on Tuesday, I replayed in my head what Sam had said to me the night before and I thought about how great it would be to live in the land of sunshine and palm trees. But by the time my phone rang the following Thursday, it no longer occurred to me that Sam might be on the other end of the line—which was just as well, because it wasn't Sam that called.

I answered the phone and waited for a response. I could hear someone talking, but it was muffled and it did not sound like they were speaking to me. I waited a few more seconds and repeated my greeting, but this time slightly louder. While I could not make out what was said, I could tell that there was a conversation going on. I started feeling annoyed at the thought of a telemarketer wasting my valuable time. Just as I took a deep breath and prepared to make one final and somewhat forceful attempt to gain the attention of this rude caller who had dialed my number and kept on talking to someone else, I heard a man say he would like to speak with Shawn.

Although I was still annoyed thinking it was a telemarketer, I quickly regrouped and told the caller that I was Shawn. The man's tone changed completely when he asked me how I was doing. I was still wondering who he was and if he was trying to sell me something, when he laughingly blurted out, "This is Ben, by the way." I was caught off guard by the phone call, yet regardless of why he was calling, I was happy to hear from Ben. We talked for a few minutes before he said that Sam had told him I was job hunting and the company he worked for now was looking to hire someone for business development. Ben added that Marcus thought I would be a good match and also said the hiring manager wanted to see my résumé.

I did not understand why the hiring manager was interested in me since Ben only knew me as a hotel valet. When I asked him about it, he told me that management had been looking for someone who was not afraid of hard work—someone with a positive attitude who would devote themselves to growing the business. When Sam told Ben I was looking for my first career position, Ben immediately remembered my work ethic and tenacity and thought I would be a great candidate for the job. Ben had shared all of this with the hiring manager and told her that I was about to graduate with a Bachelor of Science degree.

By this point, my head was spinning. Ben gave me the information to submit my résumé and also provided his contact information. I told him I would get my résumé to them the next day and expressed how grateful I was to both him and Marcus. Once I hung up the phone, I sat down to gather my thoughts and decide what to do next. In thinking about it, I realized that it was the seeds I planted as a valet that were bearing fruit far more sweet than I could ever have imagined.

I dashed off a cover letter and résumé and by that afternoon, I had faxed it to the hiring manager. From that moment on, the process seemed to happen quickly. Since I was in Ohio and the company was in California, the following week, I had the first of two phone interviews. The hiring manager and the department manager learned about me and I learned about the company and the position. Although this job was not related to my field of study, I felt it was a great opportunity. It was also my chance to get away from the cold Ohio climate and move to beautiful sunny California!

Another week passed and I had my second interview, this time with the department manager and the vice president. The more we talked about the job and what it entailed, the more excited I became. That same week, I received my diploma. I had achieved exactly what my parents had sent me to the U.S. to accomplish. It was such an important milestone for me. It also meant that I was no longer tied to Columbus. I was free to go wherever an opportunity was present.

By this point, Reza had moved again and was now living

in Southern California. He had left Ohio four years earlier and I missed him—and I missed having family nearby. When I told Reza that I might have a job in Orange County, he immediately invited me to stay with him until I found a place of my own. All of this had a big influence when it came time to decide about my future.

I was not having much luck finding a full-time job in Columbus that interested me. I came to understand that whether or not I ended up working for the company in California, whatever job I found would most likely require me to move out of the Columbus area. Since Reza lived in Orange County, and at that time, corporate jobs were plentiful and unemployment was very low there, it all meant that I would have more opportunities to find the job that was right for me.

When the hiring manager called me to schedule my next interview, I explained that I would be moving out there in about three weeks. So, we scheduled an interview for a date that fell after I would arrive and I focused on moving halfway across the United States.

This move was exciting for me. It was far different than when I moved from Indianapolis to Columbus. I was relocating to a completely different part of the country, and more importantly, I was transitioning from being a full-time college student with a part-time job to being a college grad at the start of my full-time career.

As I was driving more than halfway across the country towing a U-Haul trailer in back, it felt as if all of my experiences up to that moment had been packed in a big bundle and tucked neatly away. I was rolling into a whole new world—and I was ready to take my life to the next level.

Choosing to believe in myself and in my ability to find

work, and move to California before I was certain I even had a job, was a leap of faith on my part. So, I gladly accepted Reza's offer to stay with him temporarily, and enjoyed every moment we were together. He was also excited that we had reunited and were now living in the same area.

During the drive to California, I spent time thinking about my future. Now that I had achieved one of my largest goals, what new challenges should I focus on? I was nervous about the move, too. The cost of living in California, especially for housing, was far higher than in Ohio.

I also thought about the job I was interviewing for once I arrived. It wasn't a standard entry-level position. It wasn't even in my field. From what I knew from the first interviews, Ben, Marcus, and the people I interviewed with thought I could handle the work. I felt it was a chance for me to prove myself and earn more by doing so. However, even if I was offered the job, what if I could not do it? What if I was being naïve to think I could take on such a challenge? At times, the fear of failure grew bigger inside me with each passing mile, but I would think about how much I had gone through to get to that point and how many victories I had along the way. Focusing on these positive things helped me to remember that I am far stronger than I was when I came to America, and just like with earning my degree, I needed to remain optimistic and be relentless in pursuing my goals.

Despite the difficulties involved with moving from Ohio to California on short notice, everything went smoothly and I settled temporarily at Reza's home in the land of beaches and sunshine. Within a few days of unpacking, I was heading over to the company for what would be my first in-person, and hopefully, final interview for the job.

I met with the president of the company last. We talked numbers and discussed my work experience, the company, the job, and the market at length. Each of us spoke openly about our concerns and our expectations. By the end of our meeting, the president offered me the job and I accepted it without hesitation. He added, "As long as you work hard and use common sense, you will have nothing to worry about working here." I knew what I was responsible for and what was expected of me. Equally as important, I knew that I was up to the challenge!

The position involved heavy traveling within the southern California region, and intense pressure to increase the business level. Since I did not know the surroundings, and had zero experience in manufacturing industrial equipment, my challenge was at its peak. Here I was, already moved all across the country, with high bills to pay, and high expectations from my employer. Fortunately, my immediate supervisor was very understanding and motivating. He kept reassuring me about my potential and the ability to earn extra bonuses and potentially much higher annual compensation. I began to think how being fearful was going to affect my performance and confidence in myself. Therefore, I followed a positive mentality, and began focusing on what I knew best; work hard with a great attitude, and not being afraid of failures.

6

UNFORESEEN TWISTS

As the first year went by, I was able to contribute to the business, and made a great living. I was able to buy a brand new condominium, and a nice car within that time frame, and began living the dream. At that point, my parents were able to come and visit regularly since I had gotten their permanent residency cards, which added to my joy in every way. I had my brother and parents and friends all in one place, and life could not be any better.

This is where I want to point out that life is not always perfect, and there are ups and downs at every turn. Just when you think all is horrible, a new opportunity comes when you keep at it, or when you think all is perfect, then something happens to destroy that perfection. As this famous saying goes, "success is not final, failure is not fatal, but it's the courage to continue on that counts."

> **"Success is not final, failure is not fatal, but it's the courage to continue on that counts."**
>
> —Winston Churchill

As I was feeling the beautiful wind of peace and harmony in my professional and personal life, my mom got very sick. At the same time, our operation began expanding too fast, and invested in a large manufacturing facility. The increased overhead expenses led to the bankruptcy of the business within a two-year time span, which led to everyone losing their jobs, and the owner losing his total investment!

There I was, with no job, sick mom, and major expenses to deal with. Massive amounts of fear began taking over my mind. I began searching for another job while I was taking my mom in and out of doctor's offices and hospitals. My main focus was to care for my mom's health as I did not want to lose her after all the years we had lost being away from one another. That became my number one priority, even bigger than finding a job, and keeping my dream home. Looking back at that choice, I know that I made the correct decision by displaying genuine levels of care for my loved ones unconditionally. All material things come and go, but the love and care we give our loved ones are never replaceable with anything else. When you work hard, and care about what is right, you will get to destinations beyond belief, especially in this great nation where opportunities present themselves to those who genuinely care.

I found another job within a short period within that same industry, and tried maintaining my bills, and lifestyle. The problem I encountered there was the philosophy differences between the new employer and me. I continued to be flexible with a positive attitude, but did not agree with how they did business, and left that position after two years. I know we all will come across that at some point of our lives, and it is inevitable. The best approach I learned in such situations is to move on toward a direction where I can be myself and true to others.

All material things come and go, but the love and care we give our loved ones are never replaceable with anything else.

My mom's condition worsened, and she required a lot more attention. My dad was very attentive to her, and loved her with his whole being until the very end; however, I had to take time to attend to her physician appointments, surgery, follow up, and more. After an extensive period of medical care, my mom requested to go back home to be with her other children. She told me that she did not want to die here, and wanted to go back, and her last dying wish was that I would go to be with her during her last months of life. There I was faced with another challenge.

I began thinking very hard and long about her request, and could not stop crying about the fact that she was leaving us. I thought when I left her at age fourteen, I hoped to see her again but did not know when. In this scenario, I had one last chance to be with her before we could never see one another again.

I made my decision to grant her last wish, and gave up everything that I had worked so hard for all of those years from age fourteen to age thirty, and be with her. All of my friends and family members tried to stop me. One thing I knew was that every blessing that I had gained in this great nation was due to the fact that my family created that opportunity, and made sacrifices. I also knew, if I had reached the American Dream once, that I could do it again once I returned to America.

I tried selling my home, and due to the poor economic situation, it did not sell in a timely manner, and ended up in foreclosure. I lost all of my savings and investments in that property, and went back to be with my mom. Although it was the most challenging decision, it felt so right, and seeing her happy face brings me happiness every time I think of her.

As I went back to visit my other siblings and family members after sixteen years, everything seemed so odd for me. I did not recognize half the people, and the country had changed at so many levels. All I could think about at that moment was being optimistic about my decision, and kept telling myself everything will be okay. I did not know how it was going to work out, but I kept a positive attitude going forward, so that I could survive this major change. Although I was born there, I had been away for 16 years, which were the most critical and developmental years of my life. This made it very challenging as I did not know anything about the system there and how it all worked.

In any case, I spent quality time with family that I had not seen for so many years, and had ongoing gatherings with friends and relatives every day. My mom was so happy, and seeing her face shine every time she looked at me was the greatest gift, and assured me that I had made the right decision.

Meanwhile, I had several dear friends in the U.S., who

kept in contact with me by phone and fax, and actually offered job opportunities if I decided to go back to America. I was very grateful, but my main goal was to spend as much time as I could with my mom. She managed to survive about a year or so, and her time finally came. We were all devastated to lose her, but my dad was most affected as they had just celebrated their fiftieth anniversary. Now my dad was depressed and did not want to do anything or go anywhere.

I decided to return to America since I had no jobs or resources to make a living. Before doing so, I helped my dad move into another home since he was crying all the time when reminded of my mom in their old home. That was a great move, and my dad slowly began coming out of his depression.

I contacted Reza and told him I was coming back to California, and that I was completely broke financially and emotionally. Meanwhile, two of my friends kept pushing me to join their business, and I was not sure which direction to go. I flew back to Orange County, California, and decided to take a few days to evaluate what direction to go. One friend was in Miami, Florida, and the other was in Houston, Texas. They had unique businesses and I had no clue about either. One was an automated cash register service, and the other one in healthcare.

Since I was involved in my mom's medical treatments, I had some exposure to the medical/healthcare arena already, and found caring for people to be of great interest to me. Therefore, I took the job in Houston, and moved to another brand new environment to begin another completely new career. Since my position involved interactions with physicians and healthcare providers, I was very comfortable with the idea.

> **"I will continue doing what I do with highest level of care and passion with optimism, and I'm never afraid of failure when I do everything with excellence in mind."**

Here I was again, in pursuit of my American Dream, this time in a whole new town and new professional field. I asked my friends, who were the owners of this home infusion company, to include me in their pursuit of growth of their business, and ownership. They kindly agreed, and together our teamwork began.

I am not sure how it happened, but one door opened after another, and our business flourished to a level beyond all of our imaginations. I came up with the slogan "Ultimate care beyond compare" for the company, which was truly reflective of how we all collectively cared for patients and maintenance of a decent quality of life.

The success we were all experiencing made the American Dream so real, and I was much further along in my career success than ever before. I must point out that I was not doing any magic this time around, I was simply trying to make the right choices and not being afraid, staying optimistic, working hard, relentlessly pursuing a dream, and genuinely caring for others, while doing everything in an excellent manner. All of these basic facts had shaped a force inside me that I will describe further in Part 2. I have stuck with that philosophy as it is so simple, yet so powerful when practiced in life.

As we expanded our business, we were acquired by a bigger corporation, and most of my dear partners went their separate ways. Ever since then, I have stayed and survived five more acquisitions by different infusion companies to this day. I am often asked how I have survived five different management structures, and survived 20 years within this business; and my answer is that, "I will continue doing what I do with highest level of care and passion with optimism, and I'm never afraid of failure when I do everything with excellence in mind." This mindset has never failed me.

PART

2

THE F.O.R.C.E.
TO SUCCEED

SUMMARY

My coming to America has been an emotional journey that has brought me both deep sorrow and great joy. The obstacles I had to overcome have made me the man I am today. The difficult choices I had to make each day helped form me into a person of character.

Your choices also make you who you are today. Remember that each choice you make either adds or takes away from you; brings you forward or takes you back. Sometimes we give little thought to our decisions, and perhaps we should give them more importance. Regardless of the choices you have made in the past, you always have a chance to make different ones and turn your life into the American Dream.

My marriage was an important decision. I am so grateful to have my wife in my life. She fills my heart and eases some of the pain I have in missing my family. My children each offer me not only their love and respect, but also glimpses into the future of what may become of their lives. Watching my children share with others lessons they have learned from me makes me so happy and proud. It also helps me understand that what I experienced can offer hope to others who are young and living in this country.

It is important to point out that I would not be where I am without the help and support from many people. I have learned that if I take every opportunity given to encourage and help another person, it will actually help me in the future. I have been shown this time and again. I want all of you reading this to understand the importance of other people in your life and your care for them. Throughout these chapters, I will attempt to bring in those moments for you to ponder on.

I have shared with you my story, and now I want to share how my journey may help you as you discover America anew, and find yourself at the same time. You are able to reach for the stars by reaching deep inside yourself. That is where the transformation has to begin, from the inside out. You are able to make a difference in your life and experience peace and contentment in a land where so many can only dream about.

The word "force" has various meanings. If force is a thing, it might be described as a strength or energy or perhaps coercion or compulsion. If force is an action, it is defined as making a way through or forcing someone against their will.

Force is a powerful word any way you look at it. That is why I am choosing this word to describe how you can live out the American Dream and be successful in life. In Part Two of this book, I will be using the acronym F.O.R.C.E. as an easy way for you to remember that you have the power to do this. F.O.R.C.E. stands for:

F = FEARLESS

O = OPTIMISM

R = RELENTLESS

C = CARING

E = EXCELLENCE

The following chapters of Part Two will individually focus on each of these attributes. I encourage you to read the sections of these powers carefully. There will be examples of how each characteristic has played out in someone's life.

Learn from these life lessons. Think of how you can apply them to your life.

There will also be wisdom shared through quotes of individuals who have discovered for themselves how these powerful ways can transform your life. Their enlightenment will encourage you to take the steps necessary to make changes. You have control over your choices. Wisdom helps you make the right ones that bring you success.

You may have heard the saying, "If you fail to plan, you plan to fail." This is true. While you are being equipped with the tools of F.O.R.C.E., you also want to put them into action. At the end of the following chapters,

> **"If you fail to plan, you plan to fail."**
>
> —Benjamin Franklin

you will be challenged with a question in regards to applying what you've learned. This is an important part of the process. Knowledge alone will not help you; you must act on it … or F.O.R.C.E. it.

As you, the younger generation, embodies F.O.R.C.E., there will be transformation in our country. It starts small, but will pick up speed as more and more individuals grasp the hope that F.O.R.C.E. brings to a nation that has been lacking these qualities. America has so much to offer. Knowing what to do to obtain great success in reaching the American Dream benefits everyone.

Here's your chance to turn your life around and point it toward great things. Take the step today to begin this journey. You won't be sorry. Becoming all you were meant to be is at hand. I am excited for you, because I know this is real. You can do this!

7

FEARLESS

I tend to think you're fearless when you recognize why
you should be scared of things, but do them anyway.

—CHRISTIAN BALE, ACTOR

Defining fear seems like a simple task for we have all experienced this feeling. For you, it may be facing an exam in school, or asking that special person out for a date. The definition of fear is "an unpleasant emotion caused by the belief that someone or something is dangerous, likely to cause pain, or a threat." I think the key word here is "belief."

What we believe is how we respond. Thinking that something bad is going to happen if we do one thing rather than another, we will likely be very hesitant to go forward with it and may not even do it at all. Fear drives avoidance. Avoidance drives stagnation. If we choose to live in fear, we will never grow to our full potential. We will never experience the American Dream.

I still remember the day that Abe and I boarded that

plane for America. When I look back on it, I know it was a life-changing event that brought me to a wonderful new world with doors opening to countless

What we believe is how we respond.

opportunities. I feel tremendous gratitude to my parents for making such a difficult decision and appreciation to everyone who helped me survive the journey and make my way in America. At that time, if it hadn't been for the kind and gracious airline staff, the trip would have been a lot harder on us. It took their encouragement and care to help us through. I will always be thankful. It has also impacted me to help others who are lost and discouraged. I know what that feels like and realize the importance and gratitude felt when one is assisted.

However, I can assure you that I felt no gratitude or appreciation at the time. From the moment I awoke the morning we left Iran, the only feelings I had were of fear and sadness. My mind was filled with worry—anxiously wondering what it was like in America, what was going to happen to us, and how we would get through anything without our parents there to guide us and keep us safe.

My parents were fearful in sending us to the United States on our own with no guarantee of what would happen to us. They didn't know when and if they would see us again. They made the choice to send us for they believed more in the great things that could and did happen to us.

I was so fearful of leaving my family, country, and everything I knew, to go to a place where I couldn't speak the language. In the beginning, I did not want to go, but thankfully my parents made sure we did. My life would not be anything like it is today if I hadn't gone. I might not even be alive if I hadn't gone to America.

On the plane, not only was my mind gripped by fear, but my body, too. My face flushed, my chest was heavy with labored breathing, and sweat poured from my brow. When the plane began taxiing the runway, my body trembled, and during liftoff, it felt as if I was swallowing a baseball. Fear wasn't only a voice in my head, it was a terror that took over my entire body.

Those moments were so different from the way I feel about it now. Why? The answer is fear. It was the driving force as that day unfolded. It took hold of my mind and body, and there was little I could do to stop it.

What triggered the fear in me? Fear of the unknown. Would I be able to handle whatever came my way without the help of my parents being present? I didn't know if I could do it, especially the way I was feeling at that moment … helpless and scared.

Understanding fear is important. Fear is a necessary response to perceived physical or emotional danger to protect you. Healthy fear stops you from doing things like running into a busy street, grabbing a hot pan with your bare hands, or reaching out to pet a growling dog.

In some ways, those basic fears can be looked at as "common sense," but not all fears seem to make sense. There are those that can hold you back from succeeding in life and even cause you to sabotage your best efforts.

What we call fear can be labeled in three distinct parts:

✔ **FEAR** - a response to a clear and present danger,

✔ **ANXIETY** - a response to an unknown and/or future threat,

✔ **Stress** - the body's physical response to fear
   and anxiety.

When you experience fear, naming it is usually easy.
Many people are afraid of snakes or spiders. Others might be
afraid of flying or speaking in public. While a person may not
understand why they fear these things, what they fear is very
clear. This makes it easier for a person to at least attempt to
avoid the thing that triggers their fear.

The cause of anxiety, on the other hand, is usually
unclear. Without a specific and immediate threat to avoid or
eliminate, anxiety can be difficult to address. Feeling anxious
often has to do with the idea that "something" bad might
happen in the future. Anxiety can also be experienced when
we knowingly or unknowingly relive fearful experiences from
our past. Wilfred Bion, a psychoanalyst in the early 1900s,
coined the term "nameless dread" to describe feelings of
anxiety.

The third component, stress, is the response of your mind
and body when you feel fear or anxiety. The most commonly
known reaction is the fight-or-flight response. This is the
nearly instantaneous reaction your body experiences when you
feel any kind of threat—mental, physical, emotional, or even
spiritual. On an unconscious level, your mind will evaluate
the seriousness of the threat, decide whether to prepare to
fight or prepare to flee, and flood your body with adrenaline
and other hormones that allow you to react quickly and with
maximum strength, both needed whether you are about to
enter combat or run away.

This is what I experienced that day I boarded the
plane. I was consumed with fear as I prepared to leave my

family, and my body prepared to face the impending danger. Adrenaline raced through me, increasing my heart rate and blood pressure to drive blood throughout my body, turning my face red and causing me to sweat. I began breathing rapidly, taking in more oxygen and sending it to my brain to increase alertness. Epinephrine caused my body to release glucose and fats into my bloodstream supplying my body with extra energy.

An article written by the University of Minnesota[1] describes the effects of fear on the mind and body. They recognize that fear can be helpful to us in surviving danger, but living in fear can affect our body in several ways. It can be damaging to the heart with the constant strain of fear. Our stomachs can also be problematic with irritable bowel syndrome and ulcers.

Fight-or-flight is a response that evolved to help us survive life-threatening situations. Unfortunately, we can experience this response in situations that are not truly life-threatening. In reality, my life was not in danger when boarding that plane; however, my body reacted as if it were. My thinking was affected by fear. Immediate reactions to the fear replaced rational thinking. The fear was seen in a negative manner and my response was created through that thinking.

An important thing to know is that when we experience this response, it takes at least 20 to 30 minutes for our body to return to its normal state. That can be a long time and much can happen within that timeframe. Hurtful words can be said, physical pain can be inflicted, and opportunities can

---

[1] "Impact of Fear and Anxiety," University of Minnesota, http://www.takingcharge.csh.uPat-mn.edu/enhance–your–wellbeing/security/facing–fear/impact–fear (Sept. 30, 2013).

be destroyed. Violence can occur because of this. Perhaps someone coming into the house is thought to be a burglar, so the owner fights them by either shooting them or harming them in another way. The person injured turns out to be a family member. This could happen because rational thinking was replaced with fight or flight syndrome.

In flight from a fearful occurrence, the person runs away never really discovering why they are afraid. While in some situations, this may be a good thing, in others, they may lose an important opportunity for them. Here's a simple example; someone is afraid to go to a restaurant because the food is different and they are afraid they won't like it or it will make them sick. Not trying the food could be a missed opportunity of experiencing new things that may enhance their life. The food they are not trying could be a favorite of theirs and they don't know it. Their fear is holding them back.

I know of a woman named Katrina who discovered she had breast cancer. She was fearful not knowing what to do next. Feeling perfectly fine, it was hard to fully grasp that she had cancer. No one in her immediate family had breast cancer. Why her? She had a very public job being a leader. She had to tell her husband, her sister, other family, and the people she led. Fear made her want to disappear. She had a fear of death, telling others, and their reactions, and the change it would mean in her life. Katrina feared the surgery and treatment that followed. Would she stop living a normal life? Her answer was no. Her inside strength came out to help her when she needed it.

She approached each day with thankfulness for being alive. As a writer, she continued her work, and rested when needed. As her appearance changed with loss of hair, she continued to appear as a leader. Cancer was not going to beat her down; that was her mantra. She lived each day with joy and was able to help new cancer patients as they struggled with their new reality.

Katrina learned many things during her cancer journey. Appreciation and gratefulness for all people along with the beautiful world where we live. If she gave into the fear, her story would look quite different with many dark days. She reached her goal by choosing to be fearless.

So you have heard the implications of fear and a couple of stories from those who have overcome it. What does that mean for you? How can you overcome fear when you face it?

Learning how to reframe your thinking about fear will help you achieve so much in life. You want to control fear, not have fear control you.

> **You want to control fear, not have fear control you.**

Geoffrey James wrote a powerful article for Inc. magazine entitled "4 Mental Tricks to Conquer Fear"[2] (July 30, 2012). In the reframing process, James feels that if a person could "value courage more than security," they would be able to refocus their mental energy to what they need to accomplish and

---

[2] James, Geoffrey, "4 Mental Tricks to Conquer Fear," http://www.inc.com/geoffrey-james/how-to-conquer-fear-4-mental-tricks.html, (July 30, 2012).

move ahead, rather than focus on what they have and don't want to risk losing. Next, he suggests that one identify if the fear is real ("prudent") or not. If the fear comes from an almost certain outcome of our actions such as putting someone in danger or breaking the law, then that fear is real. However, if the fear is more of a risk issue, then discernment needs to be made whether the risk is responsible or not. James next suggests "treating fear as a call to action." When the fear arises, brainstorm what you can do to face it and make a plan. Lastly, he suggests thinking of fear as an "exciting" opportunity. He uses the illustration of a "roller coaster." It's scary when you get on, but what a ride! If a person doesn't face fear at all, they are not growing as a person and their life is most likely dull. It is in overcoming the fearful challenges that brings much excitement and appreciation for life.

Overcoming fear is an important way to achieve the American Dream. Being fearless, in a good way, will bring you places you never thought you would be. It has done that for me and I know it will for you, too.

So let me ask you a few F.O.R.C.E. questions to help you get started in living without fear. Please take these questions to heart and truly think about what your answers would be while taking steps needed to achieve your goal. The American Dream … it is real … it is yours.

LIVING FEARLESS

▲ What is your number one fear right now? Can you name it or is it a "nameless dread"? Is it a real fear or imagined? How do you know?

▲ Are you ready to take this fear out of your life so you can move ahead? If so, face the fear and find the reason it gives you fear.

▲ Replace the fear with courage. Make courage to overcome this fear more important than the fear itself.

▲ Write out the steps of how you are going to overcome the fear using the material from this chapter.

Record your results. If needed, rework your plan. Don't give up!

8

OPTIMISM

Doubt is a killer. You just have to know who you are and what you stand for.

—JENNIFER LOPEZ, ACTRESS & SINGER

Optimism is defined as "hopefulness and confidence about the future or the successful outcome of something." You may have heard about "the cup half full or half empty" thinking. If you are optimistic, the cup is half full ... you have more to drink. If you think negatively, the cup is half empty and you only have a little left to drink. Even though the amounts are the same, the attitudes are different. When you consider life, the half-full and half-empty idea can be an indicator of your feelings of your life. Do you focus on your young life being half-over in regards to being young and now you are nearing the end of your childhood and have to think like an adult, or do you think about your young life with excitement with all the things you will be doing and experiencing as you grow into an adult? Do you see how one is a lot more motivating than the other?

Olympian Kerri Walsh Jennings knows the value of optimistic thinking. When she is on her game, she knows what she needs to reach the gold. She said in an article in Yahoo Beauty, "There are a few things I do whenever I'm feeling insecure. First, I'm a big believer in positive self-talk. If you want to find the negative in yourself, you will—so I focus on the positives. My uniform is a bikini and I've learned to feel empowered by that. I have to be strong to play my sport, and I'm proud of my body for giving me the ability to compete at the highest level. Second, I focus on what I can control. I know that I can control what food I eat to fuel my body and how much effort I put into training, so I am really mindful of those things. It's also about knowing when your body might just need a rest."[3]

Most things that happen in our life are out of our control, but the two things that we can regulate are our actions and reactions. When something bad happens or plans do not turn out the way we hoped, it is normal to feel unhappy, discouraged, or mad. What can hurt you is having those thoughts spiral out of control and cloud your thinking. Getting caught in a negative thought pattern and losing sight of your goals can weaken your self-confidence, ruin your momentum, and stop you from achieving your dreams.

It is important to understand that emotions are normal. So if you try to bury them, ignore them, or beat yourself up for feeling them, it will only make things worse. If you do not process the emotions in a healthy manner, you will

[3] Yahoo Beauty, https://www.yahoo.com/beauty/olympian–kerri–walsh–jennings–believes–in–the–118461065868.html.

experience them in an unhealthy way. You will become like a time bomb that could go off at any time. If someone says the wrong thing to you, BOOM! If something goes wrong during your day, BOOM! Much damage can be done by these explosive moments. It is better to take the reins of your emotions and process them. By accepting your emotions and working through them, they often fade away.

To change how you react to a negative event, you start with recognizing and acknowledging your thoughts and feelings as normal without acting on them. Give yourself a set amount of time to work through those feelings freely and without guilt. The amount of time you allow depends on the intensity of the emotions. When that time is up, you will be ready to get back on track and continue moving forward toward your goals.

When I have negative thoughts and emotions, I might only need thirty minutes or an hour; other times it might be four hours, eight hours, or occasionally, a whole day. I have also realized that if I write down whatever pops into my mind during this time, I usually feel better faster and get back on track before the time even ends. This process will help you stay positive and keep working toward your goals with nothing holding you back.

In my journey in living in America, if I wasn't optimistic, I would have been in trouble. It would have been too easy to put my hands up and say, "This is too hard. I can't do it." I am thankful that I didn't. That doesn't mean I didn't have bad days. I had plenty of them. I remember being picked on, teased and beat up in school. I didn't understand why they were treating me this way. It hurt so much. I wanted to give up.

Because I was respectful to people, there were those in my class that took a step toward being friendly to me and helping me through the tough times. They wanted to be my friends and support me in learning about English and other American ways. Allowing me to hang with them brought me so much confidence. These are lessons I use to help others who are feeling separated.

Each of us faces different challenges and barriers, especially during high school when everything feels so extreme—so black or white. You may experience something in life that feels like a mountain to climb or a dead end with nowhere to go. You might want to give up believing you are not good enough or powerless. It's not true. You have hope and are worth it.

EFFECTS OF OPTIMISTIC LIVING

Did you realize that your attitude, either positive or negative, has an impact on your health? We are a society trying to be physically fit and sometimes totally forget that emotions play a large part of our fitness. According to the University of Rochester Medical Center[4], optimism has a great impact on health. After conducting 80 studies on living with an optimistic attitude, it found that all the participants living positively were healthier than the ones who were negative. The study covered "overall longevity, survival from a disease, heart health, immunity, cancer outcomes, pregnancy outcomes, pain tolerance, and other health topics."

[4] "Can Optimism Make a Difference in Your Life?" https://www.urmc.rochester.edu/encyclopedia/content.aspx?ContentTypeID=1&ContentID=4511, (2016).

It makes sense to take the time and energy to transform your mind from negative to positive thoughts. Think about your social life. Do the people you hang around with have a bad or good attitude? What effect does that have on you do you think? You may have found yourself reflecting the bad attitude of a friend you are with a lot. It would be difficult not to do that. It's like when a person from the northern states visits the southern states and hears him or herself begin to speak with a drawl. Our environment affects us more than we know.

Others' thoughts and feelings can rub off on you. If you have a friend who is negative about everything, don't be surprised if you start feeling a similar way. Your environment affects you. If you are in the habit of being with negative people, it might be time to consider a change for your own good. You may have noticed that people really don't like being with negative people and prefer the positive feelings of those with great attitudes. Test it out and see if this isn't true.

If one has a negative outlook on life, they will struggle more than the positive person. Everything will be harder for them. This is because they believe ideas such as: life is a waste of time for nothing good comes from it, they are the victim in any situation, they aren't good enough, people are mostly bad and want to cheat you, etc. Pretty bleak, isn't it? The stress they create in their minds is unhealthy in all aspects of life including their health and social life. They will have a difficult time achieving any goals they may have entertained. Negative people are held back by their own prisons from living life to the fullest. It's really sad to see someone living in this manner.

How to Live a Positive Lifestyle

To become a positive person takes practice, especially if you have lived on the negative side of things. Remember to be patient with yourself. New habits take time to grasp. Keep the new habit of thinking positive in front of you every day. If it takes notes to remind you or maybe writing a positive statement on your screen saver, do what is needed to transform your mind to the positive.

Let's say for example that a job you really wanted wasn't given to you. Some of the negative ideas you may have are as follows:

▲ I wasn't good enough.

▲ They hated me.

▲ The person they hired was a friend of the boss.

▲ They didn't give me a chance.

Now if you were to take one of those negative thoughts captive (stop letting it run your emotions), and really thought about it, you would most likely see the falseness of those thoughts. Those thoughts didn't really make you feel better, in fact, they may have made you feel worse.

Turning the experience into a positive one can form ideas such as:

▲ I wasn't the right person, and that's okay. There are other great opportunities for me.

▲ They were very nice to me. I enjoyed our talk.

▲ I am sure the person they hired has the skills they were seeking. I am happy for them.

▲ I am thankful for the opportunity to interview with them.

While you are practicing this throughout your days, don't get down on yourself when you forget. When you forget to put an event in a positive manner, just stop and begin turning it around in your mind until you see the truth. You will feel better about it and be set free from the lies. The more you do this, the easier it will be to do, and the more you will be able to go forward in life.

Everyone feels they are not worth anything from time to time. That is normal. The media plays into those weaknesses by trying to sell us a product that will "change our lives for the better." It's a lie. Just because someone drives a certain car, wears a new perfume, or a brand name pair of jeans, doesn't mean that their life will be all grand with lots of friends all around and fun each day. Life just doesn't work that way. Life is hard and it takes strength deep inside us to rise over the negative and walk in the positive.

Young people need to know now that it would be a mistake to focus on what the world says is success. The world says success means living in a large house, being super thin and gorgeous, having a lot of money, and never having anything to worry about. These things are nice, but they don't mean success. Just ask rich people how happy they are each day. Each person needs to discover what success is to them and then reach for that goal. This fact is important because there can be a lot of negative feelings inside you if you don't match up to another's idea of success. To stay positive, you need to be aware of what your goals are and keep them in sight. Work toward them not giving any energy to others' expectations of

> **To overcome those days when you are feeling inadequacy, helplessness, or negativity, there is only one thing to do: set your sights on your goal and keep moving forward.**

you. Feel proud of who you are and keep your head up ... it is enough. America has so much to offer you.

To overcome those days when you are feeling inadequacy, helplessness, or negativity, there is only one thing to do: set your sights on your goal and keep moving forward. Even if people around you are trying to hold you back, know that your goals and abilities are not defined by others. Only you can decide what you are capable of accomplishing, and you are probably far more capable than you think. Give yourself more credit for all you have done and what you will do in the future. Also, if you see someone struggling with negative feelings, help them turn those into positive ones through what you have learned in this chapter. Remember, being kind to another will return great rewards to you.

Go deeper now by answering the following questions. They will help you apply optimism to your life.

SAY YES TO OPTIMISM

▲ Would you say that your attitude is more positive or negative? Why?

▲ If you consider your negative thoughts, where do you think those ideas came from in your history?

Can you pinpoint the time you began to feel this way (i.e., parents were negative, friends influenced negative thinking)?

▲ When you are feeling negative, what helps you become positive again?

▲ Could you commit to saying only positive statements for 24 hours? 48 hours? It is said that if we begin by saying it, at some time we will believe it. Journal your feelings as you do this exercise.

▲ What blocks you from becoming positive? What steps could you take to overcome the blockages?

▲ What would you say to a friend who is experiencing negative thoughts? How would you help them?

You are one step closer to becoming a more positive person! You can do it!

9

RELENTLESS

There have been so many people who have said to me, 'You can't do that,' but I've had an innate belief that they were wrong. Be unwavering and relentless in your approach.

—HALLE BERRY, ACTRESS

When you want something bad enough, you become relentless in achieving it. Relentless is defined as "oppressively constant; incessant." Think about how a squirrel wants to get the food in a bird feeder. The owners of a bird feeder become quite creative in trying to keep squirrels out of the feeder from having them automatically shut when the weight of the squirrel lands on the perch, greasing the pole, and other methods. But the squirrel is relentless and will do acrobatics to get the food from the feeder. Most of the time, the squirrel wins.

That's how you need to be in achieving your goals ...

relentless. Each problem that blocks your way to victory is a challenge for you to overcome. In a way, you do acrobatics to get past the obstacle. You go out of your comfort zone to move forward toward victory. It may not be easy, but you push through because you are keeping your eye on the prize. Anyone who has played on a sports team knows the great work/pain that goes into being successful. There are practices, workouts, good eating and social habits, getting enough sleep each night and so on. That is how games and races are won. Success on a team or individual sport means being relentless.

In my story, learning English was a goal that I had to push hard on to achieve. I knew this was the only way I would succeed. So I kept that goal in front of me each day and asked for help from people around me if I needed assistance with a word. It was daunting some days, but now I am happy that I relentlessly went after that goal. English is a language one needs to know around the world, but especially if you reside in the U.S. I would not have made it near as far as I did without working every day on my English and making it my intention to learn as much as possible.

For you, it may be reading and writing skills that need improvement, or speaking clearly. Whatever it is, you can achieve it. There are people around you who are willing to help. Find them and ask. You will be surprised as I was of all the support you can get.

If you do nothing, that is exactly what you will get … nothing. Put forth the effort of making yourself better. You may reach a level you may have never considered for yourself. The spirit of relentlessness will reflect the character developed in you. It will tell a story for others to hear and be inspired by. You can make a difference not only in your own life, but others.

I also relentlessly worked several jobs to survive, go to school, and buy a car. I scrimped like a miser to do this, and worked very hard at each job There was very little time for play during those years, but it was necessary to reach my goals. Many of the jobs I worked paid minimum wage. That may seem like the hard way of earning a living, but I truly learned so much from each position I held. My focus on learning all the time kept me excited and motivated on improving myself.

I think perhaps in our society today that social media, electronic games, television (in many different modes), texting, etc. is catching the attention of many, especially younger people, and keeping them distracted from what they need to be doing such as working, studying, relating face to face, helping one another, getting involved in issues that make a difference, plus so many other worthwhile items.

Many of you may have parents that are busy providing you with a good quality of life. Part of that might mean showering you with more and more material things. While it often feels good when you first receive the latest cell phone or most popular shoes, "things" do not truly fill your hearts with joy or improve the quality of your life. What actually does is connecting with those around us. Once you know that connection is the key, you can look for ways to encourage closeness with those you care about. That might mean making it a point of spending more time with people, or it might be being more present when you are with them.

Another good thing that happened for me that came from working at all those jobs is the people I met either by serving them or being a coworker. I made sure I gave them the best service and helped them whenever possible. Serving is serving; it is important and it doesn't matter who you serve. This has helped me many times as I reconnect with people and they help me with problems or give me employment opportunities. Building your network will serve you well. Remember, people are important. Make them a priority in your life.

Malala Yousafzai, a young girl of fourteen, spoke and wrote boldly for the educational rights of female education. The Taliban was taking those rights away in her village in Pakistan. A couple of years after her story and fight came out in the media, Malala got on her school bus and was followed by a gunman who shot her three times hoping to put an end to her advocacy. What they actually did was raise awareness and support for Malala and her family from around the world.

After healing from her gunshot wounds, Malala returned to fighting for both female education and women's rights. She has been featured in Time magazine and spoke for human rights at the United Nations. Malala received the Nobel Peace Prize in 2014. She is relentless. Nothing stands in her way that she can't overcome to reach her goals.

Giving Up

Giving up is easy. You just turn around and walk away. The burden of reaching the goal no longer exists for you. You left it. You believe you are free from it. Really? What are your thoughts regarding it every day forward? Do you ask yourself "What if" questions? Just because you have left it doesn't mean it has left you. Either you will one day pick up that goal to reach again or you will be remorseful of giving up on it. That would be a sad life commentary.

Giving up can actually have an effect on you psychologically and cognitively. Your self-value may lessen if you don't keep trying to achieve your goal. Thoughts of not being good enough or a loser may infiltrate your mind causing struggles in other areas of life. Also, what you know to be true may become skewed as you reevaluate what is truth. Your goals affect every part of your life. Giving up on them will also change your viewpoint on all things, and not always for the better. When you quit trying to reach a goal, that's the death of the dream. You need to keep trying. You have a dream to be successful in this country. You want the American Dream in whatever form it means for you. It's important to you and has been a part of your life for a while now. Allowing it to die is like allowing a part of you to die. Don't let that happen. You are given one life. Make the most of that gift and become relentless in growing yourself to the best you can be. Hopefully, the following suggestions on how to stay relentless will help you.

How to stay relentless

▲ Commit to yourself that you will not give up or make excuses. When it comes to finding reasons to not do what we promised to do, we are quite creative creatures. It seems so easy to find a reason not to fulfill our commitment. Now is the time to stop that kind of thinking and become intentional on being relentless. Follow through with the expectations you have set up for yourself.

▲ Be aware that it may take more time than expected and accept it. If you expect your goal to be reached in a week and it takes a year, you need to be okay with that. Many worthwhile goals take longer than first planned. Delays and obstacles occur that can't be helped. Don't be discouraged and quit. Feel good about the fact that you are moving ahead. Keep going until you reach the goal.

▲ Pick yourself up when the plans go astray. You may feel at some point on your quest that everything has gone wrong. You may think, *Why even try anymore?* You may even do something that sets your goal further back. Regain damage control and get back on the road to success. It is difficult to stay motivated when things go wrong. Stay tough and work through the obstacles. It will be worth it.

▲ Get rid of the idea of perfection. It's hard if not impossible to achieve a perfect outcome. If you have an idea what your goal needs to look like and it seems to change as you get closer, be flexible with the variances. Trying to make everything perfect will only lead to discouragement. You need to be content with making the goal. Do not give energy to thoughts such as, "It would have been better, if ...." Celebrate what you have accomplished, for it is a great thing. You worked hard to get there. Don't lessen the value of it all with negative thoughts of not being perfect.

▲ Find what motivates you and use that to "pump you up." Give yourself little rewards as you make it closer to your goal. These milestones are important and give reason for you to celebrate as you journey on this quest. Find ways to keep excited about your goal. Remember the initial reasons you began. Think about all the good that will come from it. Know that you can achieve it. Cheer yourself on!

▲ Focus on the goal. Keep it in front of you. Tape inspirational quotes on your refrigerator, bathroom mirror, or anyplace else you would look daily. Don't lose your vigor by forgetting about your goal. Talk to people about it. They are a great resource of knowledge and experience, and will encourage you. Learn as much as you can about it. Keep moving forward in all you do to reach the goal. It is a priority for you to reach it.

Are you self-disciplined? If not, it's time to start if you want to be relentless. You are the only one who can make the choices to do what is needed to meet your goals. No one else can do it for you. If you need to get up at 5:00 a.m. every morning, so be it.

Achieving the American Dream has never been easy. It takes work. That's what makes it so worthwhile. If it were easy, we probably wouldn't be interested. It's the challenge that entices us. Every Olympian knows this. They didn't simply walk up the few stairs to receive their gold medals without the huge amount of blood, sweat, and tears that made that victory happen. It was not handed to them and it won't be handed to you either. You have to fight for it. Interestingly, the fight for the most part is with yourself. You are the one that makes the choices that help you go forward or backwards.

PUSH UNTIL SOMETHING HAPPENS

J. K. Rowling went through very difficult times. Divorced and living on welfare, she had a hard time caring for her child back in 1994 because of lack of funds. The manuscript she wrote was rejected over and over again, but she continued to push it on to publishers. Constantly, she sent out query letters and met with publishers that would shake their heads and say, "No thank you." She could have easily become faint-hearted, but made the choice to keep going. Her goal was publication and she kept that in front of her for three years until a London publisher decided to give her first Harry Potter book a chance after his young daughter read it and loved it. The rest is history.

We see Rowling's goal met and exceeded. All the work that went into it before publication is where all the lessons were learned and the relentless spirit is modeled. Great success comes with a price. The American Dream is real and it's for you.

RELENTLESS ACTION

- ▲ When you think of the word "relentless", what images come to mind?

- ▲ In what ways are you now relentless? What could you do to become more relentless?

- ▲ For you personally, what benefits would you gain by becoming more relentless?

- ▲ What would be your first step toward becoming more relentless?

▲ Do you truly believe the goal set before you is worth your commitment to being relentless and achieving the goal?

▲ What obstacles may you come across in being relentless? How will you overcome them?

In this chapter, you have learned the importance of becoming strong from the inside out. Relentlessness serves as a constant reminder of your goal and pushing you through the times when you would rather just give up. Becoming relentless in your pursuits will aid you in gaining them. Never give up fighting for the American Dream. You are worth it!

10

CARING

My guiding principles in life are to be honest,
genuine, thoughtful and caring.

—PRINCE WILLIAM, DUKE OF CAMBRIDGE

Caring is an important part of F.O.R.C.E. It's the relational segment that shows that humans were never meant to be alone. The definition of caring is "displaying kindness and concern for others." Everyone needs care at some point in their lives. You may feel independent now, and as a young person, you might even wish that your parents didn't fawn over you so much, but they do it because they love you. It has helped make you the person you are today.

When people show care toward you, what do you learn? You understand that you have value and are worth caring for. This is the same message you give others when you care about them. Many of us simply want to know that we are not alone and that we matter. Just knowing that can help some people experience a tremendous shift in their attitude.

When you notice someone in need, lend a helping hand. Not only can you make an immediate difference in their life, even the smallest of gestures can make a positive impact that lasts a lifetime. The students who helped me were sincere and reassuring, which made me feel less alone and boosted my confidence. Sadly, so many people in the world today could use a little help. Every day, pay attention to those around you. You will soon discover many opportunities to make a positive impact on others. The more you give of yourself, the more you will realize how much you have to offer.

I've seen a person transform right before my eyes. While you simply cannot help everyone, those that you do may jump into action. I often hear that my optimism and motivation are contagious. I think that is true for each of us—including you—when you reach out to encourage others and share the positive FORCE that is within YOU!

Plus, when you help others, there is something in it for you, too! In the same way that practicing gratitude is proven to benefit a person physically, psychologically, and socially, studies have shown that assisting others can help you live a longer and healthier life. In addition to feeling happier when you are altruistic, scientists have found that it can lower your blood pressure, reduce your pain, and improve your self-image.

How to Be Caring

Carlos was a boy of about 14 and lived with his mother along with an older brother and younger sister. One night, his mother's boyfriend was banging on the door to get in. Frightened that he may harm them, his mother sent the children out the back door. They went to a neighbor's home to hide. A little bit later, gunshots were heard, and Carlos' mother was dead.

This was a shock for the small town community. Not many murders were on record.

Carlos was lost and unsure of what to do from day to day. He felt as if he were walking in a fog since the incident occurred. Some friends encouraged him to continue coming to youth group at the church. Not only was he cared for, but he learned how to care for others by going on a mission trip to South America. This impacted him greatly.

Carlos and his siblings were living with their father. He was financially challenged, so it was difficult caring for three children. Carlos' friends brought over a lot of food for them. He was greatly moved by the caring they gave them. Friends would also make sure they were invited to join them for teen events. The friendships grew and deepened for them all.

Carlos didn't have a lot materially, but he was blessed with many good friends that helped him in life as he matured. In high school, he worked part-time at a manufacturing business learning about engines and received credit for this to graduate. After he graduated, he went on to college to learn how to build airplanes. He was making it. He pushed through the horrible event that happened in his life with the help of his friends and others who cared.

This is an example of how you can care for another. No matter the age, you have the ability to make someone's day. Here are some other suggestions of how you can care about others:

▲ Offer a listening ear to someone facing challenges. Remember to keep what they tell you confidential.

Trust will be built and they will allow you to listen to them when they need to talk. Don't offer advice unless asked. The person may simply need to be heard and shown that someone cares.

▲ Are you able to help by working for them and helping with chores or other duties? Sometimes people become overwhelmed with many things, and need help to get a handle on it all.

▲ Help them feel part of the gang. When you go out for a movie or dinner with friends, invite them along. It will lift their spirits and maybe give them a distraction from constantly thinking about the problem.

▲ If they have a problem that needs professional help, encourage them to seek it. Offer to go along to give support to them.

Caring for Family

My kids taught me the importance of making one-on-one time with each of them along with having family playtime. It doesn't matter if it's time for a board game, time around the breakfast table, or time on the field—any quality time together goes a long way in strengthening our family's bond. It keeps us close and communicating.

Investing time and effort into your family is important. I realize that teenagers and young adults want to be independent and build their own lives. However, spending quality time with your family works to build an unbreakable bond with those people who have your best interests at heart. Your family is an invaluable support system and the best people to reach out to for advice. Trusting those who do not truly care about you is a common way to end up making poor choices. Trust makes a difference.

Whether the people you care about most are family or friends, having them in your life will affect you in some way and you will make a difference in their lives, too. Giving those people your time and attention is one of the simplest ways to let them know you truly care and that they truly matter. Sometimes the most prized gift you can give someone is to let them know that you value having them in your life.

DON'T CARE?

If you decide that you are number one in your life and everyone else can take care of themselves, you are in for a lonely and unsuccessful life. People know when you don't care about them and most likely will not show up on your doorstep anytime soon. Your family will become distant and you'll wonder why. What's wrong with them? Well, it may not be them; it may be you.

Even if you do care, but don't act like it, people will label you as uncaring. They need to see and experience if you care about them. You may think that people should know that if they have spent any time with you, but that's not true. Unless you demonstrate caring, it will not be picked up on.

In school or working jobs, if you have an attitude that nobody else matters except you, that will not leave good memories of you in people's minds. So when it comes to future opportunities in the workforce that schoolmates or coworkers come across, you will probably not come to mind for a good person for the job. By sending the message that you don't care about them, they will respond by not caring about you. It's human nature.

With family, it's more difficult for they are people in your life for the long run. However, if relationships were not built, or if they were destroyed, there will be little contact. This makes for a lonely and sad life. Dysfunction happens in most families, so if it was in yours, you are not alone. What you must decide is if the relationship with your family is worth letting go of the bitterness of the past. If there is constant abuse of some sort that continues, then it is wise to break away, at least until both parties allow a form of help to occur (i.e., counseling).

CARING AS A MENTOR

Another story of going the extra mile in caring comes from the receiver of care from one person who made a commitment to make a difference in a young life. Emily mentored Brandy who lived in a home for teens. Here's her story:

> When I first moved into my group home, one of the girls I lived with had a lady who took her out once a week. She told me it was her mentor. I asked, "What's a mentor?" She said, "It's someone who you talk to, hang out with, and who takes you places." I wished I could have one, too.
>
> I wanted a mentor because I didn't have anybody at home. I didn't want to hang out with

the staff at my group home. They are just here to do their jobs, which is to watch us. They're like baby-sitters. I was cool with the other girls but I don't talk to them about personal stuff. I just say "hi" and "bye." And my mom had left for Hawaii with my sister and brother.

I kept bugging Ms. Francis, one of the staff people at my foster care agency, for a mentor. I had to wait a month until one was available. One day Ms. Francis told me, "I think I have one for you. She likes going to the movies and plays." I thought we'd just talk for a few hours in my room and then she'd leave or we'd go to the park or out to eat. But my mentor Emily has been more than what I expected. She's shown me around Los Angeles and done so many special things for me. She's given me good advice and we've had really good talks. When I'm with her, I don't think about what my family is doing without me. She takes my mind off all my problems.

The first time we met we went into my room and introduced ourselves. She was smiling and gave me a hug. I liked her happy personality. We listened to some CDs she brought. We liked a lot of the same music, like The Killers and alternative rock bands like Bush and Nirvana. The next time I saw her we really talked. I told her I couldn't live with my mom anymore because we were always fighting and that's why I had moved into a group home. I said that my mom used to hit me and she would cuss at me. I felt really comfortable talking to Emily because she told me about her family, too. I liked that she was open even though she had just met me.

I started spending time with Emily every Sunday. She's a talent manager and we'd see movies with the actors she works for, like Jean Reno from *The Da Vinci Code*. We like the same movies except she doesn't like gore. She knew I liked Johnny Depp so she took me to see *Pirates of the Caribbean*.

We do something new almost every week

I was happy to get out of the group home. It gets on my nerves living with five girls who have different attitudes, which can cause arguments and fights.

When my group home plans outings, they suck. They're the same boring outings every weekend, either skating, bowling, or the movies. I've done a lot of new things with Emily. She's taken me to the Grove shopping center, the Central Library in downtown and to my first real play at a big theater, the kind of things you do with your family. That's one of the extra special things about her. She wants to show me things I haven't done before.

When I was on restriction and wasn't allowed to go anywhere for a week, she brought over a brainteaser game and we played it. When I could go out with her again, she took me to Six Flags. I was so excited because it was my first time there. The best part was that we had Flash Passes so we could go to the front of the lines. One ride didn't allow the Flash Pass so we had to wait two hours.

We laughed and joked about how one of her clients was acting crazy, saying to her, "I'm better than you. I can be a famous actor."

When she brought me home I said, "Thank you very, very much," and gave her a big hug. I told her it was one of the best times I'd had. I hardly ever got to hang out alone with my mom because there was always a sibling tagging along. It made me feel special, someone dedicating their day to me.

After I had known Emily for five months, I felt comfortable turning to her for advice. I told her I didn't like a lady who worked in my group home's office. I said that she always had an attitude with me so I chose not to talk to her, and when I had to talk to her I wanted to curse her out. Emily said, "There might be people you don't like at a job but you can't curse them out." She said, "First, you have to respect her because she's an adult. Second, you have to pull her aside and tell her. You have to try to resolve the conflict." One day I didn't argue with the lady and talked to her more nicely when she told me something. Now we're OK with each other.

Around that same time, I started getting frustrated with my group home. When I returned from visiting my mom in Hawaii for spring break, they had moved me to one of the other group homes. I was mad because they moved all my stuff without telling me. The staff was getting on my nerves, too. They wouldn't be respectful, like they wouldn't knock on my door before they entered.

I told Emily I was mad. That helped because sometimes I let my anger build up and then one day I let it loose, yelling and screaming. By talking to Emily, I didn't blow up as big as I would have otherwise.

It's hard for me to talk to my mom like that because she doesn't listen to or understand me. But I always feel like Emily is listening and she understands. She never gives me a negative response, like saying "So" or "OK, whatever."

She listens to what I'm going through.

One time Emily said she couldn't relate because she didn't know anything about the system. She said it seems hard and that she wished I lived with my mom and we could get along. I'd heard that before. Everyone I'd met in foster care, like the staff at my group home and social workers, said they wish I could get along with my mom. It doesn't mean anything coming from them because they say things like that to everybody. It meant more coming from her because I knew she meant it.

When I visited my mom last summer in Hawaii, my mom and I kept arguing. It was just like old times. I was crying a lot. When I got back to Los Angeles, I told Emily that everything went bad and I had to come back early. I told her I never wanted to go back. She said, "I'm sorry." After I told Emily, as well as my teacher and my school counselor, I wasn't as mad. When I'm around one of them, they make me forget that I'm in a group home. I feel happy to be alive. It's like the feeling you'd get if you won a million dollars. They're my million dollars.

But most of the time it isn't serious with Emily. We just try to have fun. She knows I like to read, so in November Emily suggested starting a book club. We went to Barnes and Noble and I picked out a fantasy book. It had 500 pages and I finished it in four days. For the second book, she called me to say she'd just started and couldn't stop reading it.

She's so nice to me. For my 16th birthday she gave me a vampire book, a CD, and $80. I opened the card and all this money popped out. I said, "That's too much money, Emily." She said, "No it's not." I was so happy. I spent the money on clothes because my group home doesn't give us enough money for clothing and my family doesn't support me either.

It's fun doing different activities with Emily, but that's not what it's all about. I asked for a mentor because I wanted someone to talk to. That's the real reason I enjoy Emily's company and hanging out with her. I hope she's my mentor until I'm 18. After that we can be friends.[5]

Reaching the American Dream may be for you to restore relationships. People are an important part of each life. It is worth doing the work to reunite with loved ones. You can make it happen by initiating caring ... people will respond to you.

[5] Hernandez, Brandy, LA Youth, http://www.layouth.com/an–unexpected–friendship/

REAL LIVE CARING

▲ How have others shown care for you? How did it make you feel?

▲ How would you respond to someone like Carlos? Why?

▲ What do you fear losing if you become caring? How can you quiet that fear?

▲ What area in your life would you like to take steps in showing you care? What will be your first step?

▲ Is there a friend or family member you feel you need to show that you care? How will you do this?

▲ What is your motivation to want to be caring? How can you stay motivated?

11

EXCELLENCE

*We don't get a chance to do that many things,
and everyone should be really excellent. Because
this is our life.*

—STEVE JOBS, FORMER APPLE CEO

Excellence is in the eye of the beholder, just like beauty. It's difficult to establish the guidelines for near perfection because each of us has our own description of what it would be. Defined, excellence is "the quality of being outstanding or extremely good." Not perfect, for perfection is always out of reach. For example, you may be a skateboarding enthusiast. You want to make the perfect moves on your skateboard that are very well done. However, you always think of something more or better that you can do on your skateboard to raise the bar a little higher. You strive to be an excellent skateboarder.

In aiming for excellence, you improve yourself more than you think. It's not only the action that improves, but your self-worth and strengthening of your inner soul is enhanced. You become a model for others to do their best in all they do. It doesn't matter if they are an entertainer or a housekeeper, excellence is important. It impacts you and those around you.

There are many benefits to doing excellent work.

▲ You become known for doing your best and getting great results. People know they can count on you for getting the job done well.

▲ You are building your confidence, know-how, and patience in all you do. As success from projects you work on happens, you will see that the next challenge that comes up you will face with optimism knowing that you will overcome it.

▲ You will be able to stand on firm ground of knowing what is right and what isn't. There will be no swaying of your convictions. You will move ahead and not look back.

▲ You will become proud of yourself, not in an arrogant manner, but humbly realizing you are a good person looking to do your best. You realize that because of the people who have helped you and the opportunities given to you, you have become a person of excellence.

Often, the most difficult and confusing time in one's life is when you evolve from a child to an adolescent and eventually to an adult. You may face many choices that make it extremely difficult to stay on the right path toward excellence. It is important that you stay close to those whom you trust and know will help you to make good decisions. Surrounding yourself with positive and supportive people will act as a buffer to keep away those who are bad influences and will lead you astray with self-serving advice. Even though it may seem the right way to go or perhaps the easier or more fun way, don't do it. You will regret being distanced from excellence.

Excellence can be attained with others, too. Over the years, I've discovered that, whether it is regarding a personal or business relationship, if each person involved has a clear understanding of the other person's concerns, then both know what is most important to the other person. This helps you both discern if the expectations are reasonable. Can they truly be met? If not, then trying to meet them will set up failure. However, if the expectations are achievable, they can be met and exceeded.

Exceeding expectations can be done if a person desires excellence. It's not normal to go beyond what is expected, but to meet requirements. There is something special about someone who raises the level up beyond mediocrity. They have a strong work ethic that is to be admired. Anyone can do this if they put their mind to it. It's just making the choice to do it.

In my job, I tried to always work beyond expectations. The business volume grew tremendously as I learned my way around the business. One thing that I have learned in all these years is that people are people regardless of the industry, and as long as you work hard with a great attitude, treat people with a high level of respect and with a genuine level of care, you can be successful. Excellence includes how you work with others. Be mindful of them and ready to serve.

Everton's story of excellence

Excellence started in Everton Edmondson's story as a child. He lived in Houston, Texas most of his life. His parents gave him an incredible childhood; even though his father worked brutal schedules as a physician, he always made time for adventures with Everton. This made a huge impact in his life.

Everton always felt loved by both parents and was actually an only child the first ten years of his life. He always asked his parents for a little brother, and a decade after Everton was born came his brother, Ethan. They are still close siblings.

Everton's mother has always been incredibly nurturing and attentive. He says, "We have similar personalities. She's taught me so much and is a perfect role model for what a mother and wife should be for her family. My dad has shown me the values of hard work and providing for a family. He's also taught me how to roll with the punches in life and not take things too seriously. Both my parents succeeded in teaching me how to be a man and someday, a good father."

He chose not to become a doctor like his father. He pursued other alternatives focused on another goal. As he attended Loyola University in New Orleans, he stayed with work connected to the medical field. After a few side jobs, and wondering if he should move out of state, his dad asked him a number of times if he would work for him as a manager. The intention was to help his father's business for a short term. Everton considers it one of the best decisions he made professionally and personally. He was able to bond with his parents in a different way, seeing them both in a different light that would never have been possible without his experience in the family business. He has been a medical practice human resource manager for his father's business since 2003.

Everton describes himself as being humble, hard-working, loyal and committed to his family and closest friends. At times, he can be a bit intense about certain issues, but doesn't let it affect the way he works through a situation always striving for excellence. He is proud of graduating with a Master's degree, staying physically fit, and the contributions he has made to his father's medical practice.

After working through a painful relationship, Everton has once again found balance through weightlifting, cycling, reading, and spending time with his new girlfriend. Regaining his peace also came from the supportive relationships he has with his family and friends. Talking to loved ones always lifts his spirits. Opening up to one another, being vulnerable, and really caring about each other makes relationships real and trusting. These tactics to live an excellent life not only help him, but he is able to help others. He finds it rewarding.

Some of the things Everton would still like to accomplish are to continue to grow and expand his knowledge, skills, and abilities. Family is also a priority to him, so making sure there is time in his schedule to be with them is important. He would like to one day raise a family and give this legacy to future generations. Everton believes that to live an excellent life, one's main goal in life should be to maximize potential in all facets of life, and achieving a healthy work/life balance.

Living a life of excellence isn't difficult. Living with consistency with your beliefs of how your life should be makes it excellent. Nobody wants a life that is a waste, but somehow that is how people end up by making the wrong choices along the way.

SHODDY VS. EXCELLENCE

Shoddy quality means to have something poorly made or an action that is low quality. For example, you buy new clothes and when you wash them, the color fades and the material frays. The clothes were not made with a sense of excellence.

Another example is getting your car fixed. You pay the garage that repaired it only to find as you are driving home, parts are falling off. This is shoddy work. The mechanics either didn't know what they were doing or didn't care.

So what are your responses to getting shoddy items or service? Is that something you want to repeat? Probably not. You most likely will not purchase anything again from wherever your poor quality item came from, or return to the business that gave poor customer service. You don't want to waste your time or money. You're likely to tell others about your experience, too.

Giving bad service in any form leads to a dead end.

Nobody wants to be on the receiving end of that. So if you decide that excellence isn't your thing, then please, don't plan on growing and achieving the American Dream. It will pass you by. Here are some other things that may happen if you are not aiming towards excellence:

▲ When new opportunities arise, you will not be considered or perhaps thought of at all. People, especially leaders, want the best. The best is simply someone who works hard, respects people, and goes for the gold in all they do. That can be anyone. Will it be you?

▲ Your self-esteem will lessen because you don't believe you can do anything well, falling into your own self-made prophecy. You do less than quality work and others tell you that you can't do it right. Without really reaching for high quality, you accepted low quality.

▲ The legacy you leave for future generations will not be a positive one. Your life and work ethic won't inspire others. How do you want to be remembered?

▲ It may cause problems in your immediate family if you're not trying your hardest for them. They may feel that you don't care enough to put forth the effort. Think of how you feel when someone goes out of their way to do something for you. It feels good!

Make excellence a part of your life. The American Dream is reached by those who want to do the best they can in all instances. From the time you wake up in the morning, set your mind on being excellent. Then the decision is already made and you can go forth with that expectation of yourself. Remember, this does not mean being perfect because that is unreachable, but it does mean to live above the level of mediocrity. You can do it!

EXCELLENCE: YOUR NEW QUALITY

▲ When you think of excellence, what is the first thing that comes to mind? Why do you think that is?

▲ What do you think you have done with excellence? What areas do you think you could improve?

▲ What would be the difference in your life if you came at everything you did with excellence?

▲ What is the connection between excellence and achieving the American Dream?

▲ What will be your legacy for future generations?

▲ Think of one area in your life that you want to improve on. What will be your first step to achieve excellence?

PART 3

CONCLUSION

Summary

You have finished reading my story, the F.O.R.C.E. concepts, and now you are ready to live the rest of your life in the American Dream. It is yours ... it is real. Part Three is going to tell you how to do that every day. You will learn my secrets of staying focused on living the F.O.R.C.E. and continuing to better yourself. I do not ever want to be content with who I am. I know that I am still growing from the inside out and that better things will come my way if I stay alert, active, and assertive.

Also, I am adding a "cheat sheet" that will help you remember all you have learned from this book. It is easy to reference instead of reading through the whole book again to find what you are looking for in a subject. However, if the subject doesn't seem clear after reading the cheat sheet, you may want to go back to that section and reread it to help for your retention. The sheet will also ask questions to help you with your journey.

This is truly an exciting time for you! I applaud you in taking the steps to grasp the American Dream that is within your reach. If you keep focused and follow the direction of the F.O.R.C.E., you will make it. Only you can hold yourself back ... don't do that. Life in America has so much to offer and perhaps it takes an immigrant to fully see and understand that, but I don't want you to miss it.

My advice to you is to not delay. Start now on your new journey. Are you ready?

GETTING STARTED

Make a plan. If you are ready for living the F.O.R.C.E., you are ready to map out your commitment. Take each segment of the F.O.R.C.E. and transform it to how you will live it out. For example, FEARLESS: I, *(name)*, refuse to hold on to fear when it tries to overtake me and my plans to reach the American Dream.

OPTIMISM: I, (name), will stay optimistic each day no matter the circumstances. If I do need time to mourn a challenging day, I will do so, but set a time limit so that discouragement does not take me off-track from reaching the American Dream.

RELENTLESS: I, *(name)*, commit to having a relentless nature in regards to achieving the American Dream. I will not give up.

CARING: I, *(name)*, will care for the people around me, especially family and friends, realizing fully that each person is important and part of reaching the American Dream.

EXCELLENCE: In all I do, I, *(name)*, will give my best to both people and tasks. This level of living will help me reach the American Dream.

Write out your plan and leave a space for you to sign. This adds to the self-accountability. You may want to have someone sign as a witness who can keep you accountable, but you know what works best for you. This may seem like a silly step to some of you, but I guarantee it does help you to stay on track. Keep the commitment tacked on a wall or someplace you will see it every day. Constant reminders of your plan to achieve the American Dream keep you focused.

How to Live Fearless

You may have heard before that the best way to become fearless is to face your fears. That is somewhat true, but I will take you a step further. Facing a fear is identifying it. You know what it is as well as how you feel when it appears. You are facing it. Now it is time to transform that fear into a challenge to overcome. This takes it to another level where it will not control you.

For example, let's say you are fearful of public speaking. You know that you have always been afraid of it and it comes up every time you are asked to talk in a group. You currently avoid speaking to a group with a passion. It is controlling you. Now let's take apart that fear so we can see what it really holds. Unpacking fear will lessen it and you experience more freedom.

What do you believe may happen if you speak in front of a group? For the example, I will list a few possibilities. You may fear the following:

▲ people will reject you and what you say

▲ you will faint or become ill

▲ you will give wrong information to the group

▲ your voice will choke up

You notice that all of the above are focused on you. You can transform those thoughts by refocusing on who it is about. Public speaking is for the audience, not you. You are serving the listeners with ideas and experience. They want to hear what you have to say or they wouldn't be there.

There are some ways to calm your spirit on the above listed fears. After you convince yourself that the crowd wants to hear you, you can practice your talk. This will ease the fear of fainting or being sick, because the more you practice, the more it will seem natural for you to speak on. Share your talk with family members, friends, the dog, anyone who will listen. Your voice will not choke up with practice. It will be smooth and calm as you talk with your friends (that's how you should think about your audience, as friends).

Next, make sure what you are talking about has been researched so that you can be calm in knowing the information you share is correct. The library has people who would love to help you research a topic.

You see, there are ways to transform your fears into something powerful and effective. Becoming fearless takes some work as you process the list of fears you may have currently. It is worth it. Believe me, I would not be as far as I am if I allowed fear to run my life. Make your life a no fear zone and achieve the happiness of the American Dream.

LIVING IN OPTIMISM

Think about yesterday. List all the negative things you can think of in regards to that day. Were you angered in any way? Did you get a low mark on a test or paper? Were your friends aloof? There are many ways we can consider a day has gone bad.

When you are frustrated by something that happens in your day, what is your response? Most people hold on to the bad feelings for a while and allow them to linger in their mind. It ruins a large portion of your day, doesn't it? This is living in negativism.

Living in optimism means to always consider the good things in life, no matter what happens. Let me be clear that when great losses happen in life such as death, divorce, or job loss, a time of grieving is normal and should be done. However, you can still be optimistic. You need to believe that things will get better and live on that belief. That doesn't mean you are living a fantasy; it means that you having a positive outlook will put into action what you believe, enabling you to continue toward your goal.

This takes practice, so don't beat yourself up if you find yourself in negativity. Keep trying to see the positive. Here is what you can do to start. Take that list of negative items you created earlier, and brainstorm what a positive outlook could be. For example, let's say you received the low mark on a test. Yes, it makes you feel bad at first, but let's look at it a different way.

There are items on that test that you did correctly. You learned those things. The test has shown you where you need to grow. Perhaps it is more studying you need or more clarification from the instructor. These are very doable. The test is revealing the next steps for you, and that is a positive.

Another example, your friend seems distant yesterday, and you think it has something to do with you. Most of the time, it has nothing to do with you and everything to do with what they are going through at the time. Here is the positive. You are given an opportunity to reach out to them to show you care. You know that you can make a difference in someone's life, so you refocus your thoughts from, "What's wrong with me?" to "How can I help them?" I am sure your friend will appreciate your care very much.

Living optimistically means having the thought, "I can" instead of "I can't" at all times. It means appreciating all that life in this country has to offer and recognizing it as a gift. It is knowing that there is a solution for every challenge that comes your way.

Start practicing now. Don't waste any more time being negative for it will get you nowhere. Be optimistic and reach the American Dream.

RELENTLESS LIVING

The Energizer Bunny, it keeps going, and going, and going…. You've seen the commercials with the pink toy rabbit hitting the drum and moving on. The bunny is relentless and that's what you need to be.

Establish your goal for reaching the American Dream and keep your eye on it. Continue to move toward it never giving up, no matter what. This type of living makes you stronger on the inside. Giving up is easy; staying on track toward the goal is not.

So how do you do this? Practice not giving up. Consider the things you have given up on in your life already. Now rethink how you could have been relentless in pursuing that goal. Maybe it's not too late. What if you picked it up again and renewed your commitment using the F.O.R.C.E.? What could be accomplished by this?

Now think about your new goals. What will keep you motivated to continue working on reaching them? That is what you need to use to keep you going. Consider what your life will be like once the goal is reached. Maybe have a picture of that tacked somewhere you see each day. Look at it and remember, it is yours for the taking. You will reach it, but you can't give up. If you give up, you lose. You want to win, so be relentless.

CARING ENOUGH

Who cares about you? How do you know? Are there words or actions that tell you this? Think about how you can send the message of care to another using some of these examples. It's great to come up with some of your own, too. Again, it takes practice to get into making caring a natural response for you. Right now, it may feel unnatural where you have to think about it before you act. It will get better though.

Let's divide the people who you have the opportunity to care for into two groups: family and others, which includes friends, coworkers or schoolmates, clients, strangers, etc.) and describe ways you could show care for them. There may be a difference in your response depending on how well you know them.

Family: These are the people you see daily or often that have a direct connection with you. This includes parents, siblings, grandparents, or any other family member that is close to you. The number one way you can demonstrate your care for them is by spending time with them. This shows that you enjoy who they are, respect them, and love them.

Spending time may look like playing games together, going out for coffee, seeing a movie, cooking together, playing basketball, shopping, etc. It doesn't really matter what you are doing, but that you are doing it together.

Support of family members when challenges arise is crucial. Who else can they fully depend upon? If a family member gets sick, you make a way to care for them or coordinate help for them. If a member loses their job and has no money coming in, the family can surround them and help them get by until another job is found. Being there for the family makes you an important part of the whole.

Other things you could do are to help around the house by dusting, washing dishes, taking the trash out, and more without being asked. This will show how you are maturing into a responsible adult. You will be trusted with more as you offer more. This is a benefit to you and works outside of the home, too. As people outside of your family see how caring you are and how you follow through on your promises, they will not forget you. We'll talk more about this in the next section.

Caring for others: This is a bit different in that others normally have their own families to help care for them. Sometimes that's not the way it is for an individual, so instead of them being alone in a situation, you may choose to stand by them and help as you can. Simply being with them and allowing them to talk is a huge part.

Coworkers or schoolmates may need help with a project or situation. Maybe they have more work than they can handle and need help. You can show care to them by helping.

Also, be intentional in including them in social situations. Everyone needs to feel welcome.

There is a wariness when it comes to helping strangers. We must be wise in discerning whether or not to help a stranger. If it seems safe to do so, and there are plenty of people around, then cautiously assist them. This comes up a lot with cars breaking down. If you have a cell phone, call the police about their car rather than stopping, unless your absolutely sure it is safe.

When it comes to elderly people, they are safer and sometimes need a lot of assistance. Sometimes it's in the grocery store and they can't reach the product they need, so you could get it for them. Maybe visiting a nursing home would be something you would like to do. Visits bring a lot of joy to the people in the homes. It shows that you care.

Caring for individuals is a life-long mission that all should do. If you are living the F.O.R.C.E., it will become a natural part of you.

LIVING IN EXCELLENCE

This is what brings it all together for you. It is doing everything as best as you can. If you clean the refrigerator, do it with excellence. If you drive a semi, do it with excellence. If you are a parent raising a family, do it with excellence. If you are a student, study with excellence. It is a mindset you are creating in you that makes your first response be one of excellence.

After living with this mindset for a while, it will also become natural to you and your responses will always be given in excellence whether it is verbally or physically. Here are some ways you can begin living in excellence:

Each person you see, smile at them. This may seem quite unnatural for some of you, but you will get used to it. It shows that you are a positive and caring person. The smile will lighten their day and help make them feel better.

In your work or schoolwork, think of it as performing it the first time in your life. Be excited and desire to do the best you can do. Go above what is expected and make a name for yourself as someone who does excellent work. People do not forget the people who are good workers. When opportunities for advancement come up, you can be sure that your name will be mentioned. Everyone wants good workers around them.

There are things in this life that aren't very exciting to do; in fact, not many people like doing them at all, such as washing someone's feet during a pedicure. In the salon, it may be okay, but what about at home or for an elderly person who can't wash their feet anymore. Do it with excellence and that will show the F.O.R.C.E. being lived out in you.

Think about what excellent things you can do right now. Plan more for tomorrow. Get started and see how people respond to those of excellence.

The American Dream is reached through excellence. Mediocre doesn't make it.

The F.O.R.C.E. Reference Sheet

	Fearless	Optimism	Relentless	Caring	Excellence
Defined	"an unpleasant emotion caused by the belief that someone or something is dangerous, likely to cause pain, or a threat."	"hopefulness and confidence about the future or the successful outcome of something."	"oppressively constant; incessant."	"displaying kindness and concern for others."	"the quality of being outstanding or extremely good."
Quote	*I tend to think you're fearless when you recognize why you should be scared of things, but do them anyway.* —Christian Bale	*Doubt is a killer. You just have to know who you are and what you stand for.* —Jennifer Lopez	*There have been so many people who have said to me, 'You can't do that,' but I've had an innate belief that they were wrong. Be unwavering and relentless in your approach.* —Halle Berry	*My guiding principles in life are to be honest, genuine, thoughtful and caring.* —Prince William	*We don't get a chance to do that many things, and everyone should be really excellent. Because this is our life.* —Steve Jobs
How did you live out today?					
Areas you have fallen short					
Improvement strategy					

IT'S TIME TO START!

I am truly excited for you and the new improved way you are going to live your life and grasp the American Dream. The F.O.R.C.E. will take you places you never imagined for yourself. You are rebuilding yourself from the inside out using the concepts given in this book and the outcome will be something great!

This country holds so much promise for you. There will be opportunities for you that you didn't know existed. Don't miss them. Make the commitment to live your life with all you are and can be. ***Your goal of reaching the American Dream is real. Enjoy it!***

Additional Resources

The following people have great inspirational stories that you may find helpful in focusing on reaching the American Dream:

- Roger Staubach, the legendary NFL player: http://www. profootballhof.com/players/roger-staubach/

- Shawn Mendez, superstar among teens: http://www. rollingstone.com/music/features/shawn-mendes-how-a-toronto-teen-became-the-superstar-next-door-20160413

- Kathy Ireland, supermodel: http://www.forbes.com/sites/ natalierobehmed/2015/05/27/how-kathy-ireland-built-a-420-million-fortune/#5425bff24612

- Tony Robbins, motivational speaker: https://www.ted. com/talks/tony_robbins_asks_why_we_do_what_we_do?language=en

- Dr. Jennifer Heartstein, teens and technology: http://www. drjen.com/

- David Niven, PHD, 100 simple ways to solve problems: http://www.davidniven.com/

- Dr. Phil: http://www.biography.com/people/dr-phil-mcgraw-9542524

About The Author

SHAWN NOROUZIAN is a businessman working in Texas and has developed the F.O.R.C.E. for youth to understand and reach their full potential. He graduated from Franklin University in Columbus, Ohio. He has much experience with business development working in the medical and healthcare arenas. Shawn lives with his family, including three children who keep him busy. The love of family and people is his number one priority!

Shawn wants to remind you that we live in the greatest country where opportunities are beyond words, and appreciation of it is a must. He wants you to capitalize on every chance you are given to improve yourself by using your positive F.O.R.C.E. That's why he encourages his readers to share their experiences using any one of the F.O.R.C.E tools. Please visit his website and share your story at www.YourPositiveForce.org.

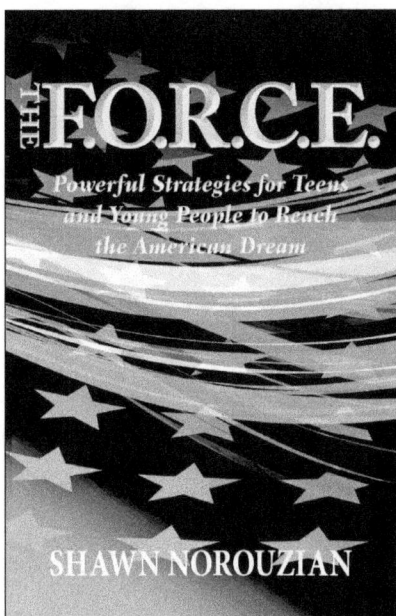

The F.O.R.C.E.

*Powerful Strategies for Teens and Young
People to Reach the American Dream*

Shawn Norouzian

Author website: www.YourPositiveForce.org

Publisher: SDP Publishing

Also available in ebook format

Available at all major bookstores

SDP Publishing

www.SDPPublishing.com
Contact us at: info@SDPPublishing.com

www.ingramcontent.com/pod-product-compliance
Lightning Source LLC
LaVergne TN
LVHW021508080426
835509LV00018B/2444